LEGALLY BRANDED
A Memoir

SHANNA RED

Artist Revolt Publications

Legally Branded Copyright © 2015 by Shanna Red

All rights reserved, except for the use of promotional purposes, reviews, or articles. This book is a work of fiction. Names, places, and incidents are the product of the author's imagination and are used fictitiously. No parts of this book shall be duplicated, reproduced, recorded, photocopied, or shared electronically, by any means now known or invented hereafter, without the publisher's written permission. By reading this book, you are agreeing to such terms. Any resemblance to actual persons, dead or alive, locales, or events is entirely coincidental.

ISBN-13: 978-1517235673
ISBN-10: 1517235677

Interior design and typesetting by: *interiorbookdesigns.com*

Published by:
Artist Revolt Publications
arpsubmissions@aol.com

I dedicate this memoir to Calib Dewberry (My Son).

Acknowledgments

Lorraine McGregor, you are the mitochondria (workhorse) that gave me courage to tackle this project. "An Eyes Journey"…indeed it has been … Thank you! Erika Williams, you saw REAL potential in me and made me work on my dreams with tough love, thank you! Su Bee thanks for being you, and helping me when I needed it the most. Damond, I will never forget those long conversations on the phone, you eased my fears…get ready for another phone call. "Brutha" Dr. Cornel West, loved your embracing hug that came along with your soft beard…keeping it "Funky (real)." Sister Debbie, I love you and thank you for seeing the best in me. George, thanks for listening to me every day while writing this book, and I hope I made you proud. Anthony and Kayle, thanks for the pep talks and the love in my green tea, while writing this book! Messiah Equiano, always Dan to me! Thank you for your positive energy and continue your love for our troubled children/youth…we need more people like you. Jennifer (Jday), I want to be like you! Elias, I want to meet you! Garrard McClendon, the voice of our communities throughout Chicago, and the coolest brother on the face of this planet…I'm encouraged! Michael Baisden, you spoke to me, and I listened. Well, you spoke to your audience, but I took it personally.

And I quote: "Write a book, and it must have purpose."

Thank you Mr. Baisden. Father Pfleiger, thank you for all that you do for our children and the community, and thanks for opening your doors to my son and I …we love you. Linda, thank you, if it wasn't for you, I wouldn't have had the opportunity to work on my book daily, I'm grateful…we love you. Sister Rochelle Cross, you have given me tools to use for life, I love you!! C. Shabazz and T. Lindsay, always there for me when I'm anxious. Thank you!! Choyce Johnson...lol, you know I love you immensely, thank you sweetheart! Martell…lol, you've given me a gift that I'll protect as long as I live, our son…thank you. Last but not least, to Calib. Son, you gave your mother a purpose to live and someone to die for. You are my reason to be the best person I could be. I love you more than the word.

"I don't handle failure well, I refuse to give up!"
Michael Lewis Plfeger

PROLOGUE

Who is supposed to care for you no matter what? Family, that's who. Well, I have a different perspective on family, and I'll start with the members of my own family. I have an older brother named Carl who is five years older. My youngest brother, Andrew, was named by the hospital at birth. I never met Andrew. He was born addicted to heroin due to our mom, Clare.

My father was Ronald Fletcher. The only knowledge I have of him came from my mother. He died of Cirrhosis of the liver in 1974 at the age of twenty-nine. My mother told me about my father and little brother when I became an adult, and only because I asked. She told me about both with tears in her eyes.

My dad was a white man who had features like the white Christ, long hair and a beard. Andrew, she couldn't describe because he was taken away from her at birth.

My grandmother, Rose, was a "church going woman." She was from the South and worked day and night, which didn't allow her a healthy relationship with my mother. She died of cancer in 1998 at the age of seventy-nine.

I have two uncles who have been incarcerated most of their lives. I had an aunt, Cynthia, who was schizophrenic and died in 1994. I know very little about my blood relatives. They were estranged. My mother, Clare, lived her life as free spirit with few family ties, and her addiction to heroin eventually cut her ties to my brother and me. She left our care to other people.

I was born on the Westside of Chicago in 1969 at Cook County Hospital, and as a child, the Westside was all I knew.

The Westside boogie is the best side boogie, and the Southside boogie ain't shit.

I loved the Westside because that was home. I was stable there for a little while, stable in the sense that I actually lived in one place and didn't move from home to home. Moving from place to place didn't happen until we: my mother, my brother, and I, left the Westside.

This moving caused me to feel uneasy and worried as a child. It started when we left my grandmother's. I didn't remember the move, but remember the after; I remember my mother leaving us in different places and with strange people. I was constantly worried because my mother was always gone.

Carl and I slept anywhere we could rest our heads when our mother left us in strange places. Sometimes, we knew the people, most times we didn't. My mother was so addicted to drugs that she didn't realize or didn't care what kinds of people she left us with.

Once, we stayed with a woman who put Carl and I out on her front porch because my mother had been gone for days. It was dark, and snow covered the cars and streets, and we were hungry, so Carl and I went to the nearest warm spot, a tavern. We walked in to warm up and beg for food. My brother did all the talking and got us some chips, pop, and heat. The bartender sat us at a back booth, and we munched liked the starving children we were.

"Don't y'all kids have somewhere to go, and where y'all momma?" A drunken lady slurred.

"We don't have nowhere to go, and I don't know where my momma is at!" Carl snapped.

The lady, a total stranger, was wearing a red and white-checkered smock. She looked at us hard and steadied her drunken self against the booth.

"Where your mama?" She asked again.

Neither Carl nor I answered. She yelled something to the bartender and walked away. A little while later, she came back, and for reasons unknown to us, she took us to her home and gave us shelter and a warm place to sleep.

The woman's name was Beth. She was a mean, skinny, wig-wearing witch of horror. The next morning, she woke us up with breakfast. But, when she saw the piss wet mattress, her concern changed.

"Who pissed on my mattress?"

Me, being the youngest, her accusing eyes went to me, and I was automatically blamed. I looked at my brother, knowing he had wet the bed, but he did not say a word.

"Don't piss in my bed nomo, I'ma let you get away with it the first time. What's yo' name?" She asked with a cigarette hanging from the corner of her lips.

"Shashanna, and I'm telling my momma on you!"

"Yo' momma ain't here, and she shouldn't had left y'all ass in da Tavern in the first place!" Beth yelled.

"Shashanna, be quite befo' she put us out," Carl whispered.

"I don't like her!" I said with my arms folded tightly.

"Shhhhhh!" Carl gestured with his finger pressed to his lips.

After she fed us, Beth started asking questions about my momma while making phone calls. Carl answered most of the questions while I just stood looking at the mean lady and listening to her talking on the phone about my mother.

The Transitions Begins

I was four years old and in a strange place without my mother, and with a lady who was mean and spoke of my mom in a derogatory manner, which made me want my mother more. I wanted to yell out, "I miss my mom! I miss my mom! I miss my mommy!" No one knew where my mother was, and so we stayed with the witch that picked us up from the tavern, Beth.

She officially became our guardian. We lived with Beth's mother and her two grandchildren. Beth's mother, Granma, wore old wigs and cat-woman framed glasses. The first time I saw her with her wig off, I thought she was a strange man who had snuck into our house until she started talking and put the wig back on.

Granma's two grandkids, Nancy and Lance, were older than Carl and me, and six of us lived in her two-bedroom apartment. I didn't know if the apartment was home, or if my mother was coming to get us. I knew I missed my mother and was tired of hearing Beth say things like, "Good women don't leave they kids on the streets." Carl and I were in a new place where we ate and were warm, but my mother was gone, and I was four years old and always worried.

Beth, who talked bad about my mother leaving us, was never home. She worked all the time, and my brother was in school, and Granma would go out and babysit. Leaving for work and school left me alone with Granma's crazy grandson, Lance.

Lance was a really weird fat kid, and I never felt good being alone with him, even before he started torturing me. When everyone would leave, Lance would whip me with hangers, belts, burn me with fire and make nooses out of scarves. He would put the scarf noose around my neck and hang me from a hook on the back of the door. I would gag and gasp for air while crying.

He would watch me suffer and laugh hysterically. When he thought I had enough of his torture, he'd take me off of the door hook and threaten me, and he would order me not to tell anyone. I don't know how long this shit went on, but I dreaded the weekdays and welcomed the weekends because everyone was home, and Lance couldn't hurt me.

I remember looking out of the window a lot, and daydreaming that the little girl outside playing was my sister. Somebody would put a radio in the window while she played outside. The day I met her, the radio was playing the song, "Rock The Boat."

She danced so freely to the song and sang so joyfully, *"Rock the boat. Don't rock the boat, baby. Rock the boat. Don't tilt the boat over. Rock the booooooooat."*

When I think of Bridgette, this is what I remember first. Eventually, we met and became friends. We played rope and hopscotch. She only lived a couple of doors down, so we saw a lot of each other.

Early on, I almost ended our friendship due to my insecurities. Since I had a lighter skin complexion and longer hair, the other kids on the block called me a white girl; Bridgette didn't, but being teased by the children, only added to my worries, and I wanted the teasing to stop, so I cut my hair. I wanted to have an Afro like most of the other kids.

Beth came home and yelled, "What happened to yo' got damn hair?"

I panicked and said, "Bridgette cut my hair."

Immediately, Beth took me to Bridgette's house and confronted her and her Mother.

"I didn't cut huh hair. She's telling a story on me!" Bridgette protested.

I felt guilty, but I stuck to my story, and Bridgette stuck to hers.

"Somebody's lying!" Beth said while pointing her finger at Bridgette and me.

"Well, if Bridgette said she didn't do it, she didn't!" Bridgette's mother said with conviction.

The two adults started to argue. I felt bad, but I didn't want to get a whipping. Beth cursed Bridgette's mother out and took me home.

As soon as we walked through the door, she asked, "Bitch, is you lying on Bridgette? What da hell happen, tell me da truff!"

She began looking for a belt or an extension cord. I knew this because of the frantic way she was looking around. This was how she acted when she was getting ready to whip a kid. She threw around couch cushions and yanked open dresser drawers.

"I aint telling a story!" I cried.

Beth found the extension cord and struck me a couple of times.

"You ain't telling the truth, you lyin'!" Beth said while bringing the extension cord down across my young thighs.

"I cut my hair! I cut my hair! I cut my hair!" I confessed to stop the whipping.

"What the fuck you lie on that girl fuh? Where is da hair, Shanna!"

I walked into one of the two bedrooms and got my hair from behind the radiator and showed it to her.

"I cut my hair hoping to stop the kids from calling me white or a honkey."

"You made me cuss that girl and her mother out for nothing, and now I'm about to really whup yo' ass!"

I immediately braced myself. This wasn't the first whipping Beth had given me. My Mother never beat Carl and me. But Beth whipped us like runaway slaves. The ironing cords left red welts all over my body and etched into my mind a lifetime hatred for the woman.

On weekdays, Carl went to school and then outside to play, so I hardly saw my brother, and I missed him. He seemed to be adjusting to the new environment just fine, whippings and all. Beth was always giving him things, and she allowed him more freedom. Once she gave him a BB rifle that shot metal pellets, and he loved it.

We were on the porch playing with the rifle when he asked me to, "Hold up yo' hand."

Which I did, and he shot it, right in the center. I wailed because it felt like a match was in my palm.

"Be quite, be quite, here."

He handed me the gun, and covered up my mouth. He let me shoot the rifle off the back porch for a while, but he should have let me shoot his ass in the hand like he did me. I liked the gun, but Carl wouldn't let me keep it.

I had gotten tired of Lance's weird abusive shit, and I figured the rifle would help me, but since I was too afraid to tell Carl why I wanted to keep the gun, he wouldn't let me keep it, but the very next time Lance tried to wrap a scarf noose around my neck, I ran out of the house screaming. Neighbors came, and asked me what was wrong, and I told them what Lance had been doing to me. One of them told Beth, and Lance got his ass whipped right in front of me. My daily tortures were over. Lance said he hated me, but he never touched me again.

My new foster family moved, but Nancy and Lance didn't stay with us very long because their mother found a place. Our new place was dirty, dilapidated, and rat infested, and when I say rats, I mean "super rats."

Big rats that dared us to move out of beds at night. I was so scared. When the lights went off, I didn't move for anything. We could hear them walking across the tile and wood floors; the clicking of what Carl called "rat toenails" was heard nightly. In our new raggedy ass apartment, we had everything that was nasty: water bugs, roaches, mice, and rats. There were so many mice and rats that Carl would shoot them with his BB rifle.

We had three bedrooms, a living room, dining room, and a raggedy ass kitchen. One of the bedrooms was used for storage because the people that lived downstairs told us that someone died in the room before we moved in. Granma made a makeshift bedroom out of a space that was connected to the dining room.

I slept with Granma who snored so loud that it took me forever to fall asleep. Not only did Granma snore, she had a piss can on the side of the bed to avoid leaving the room at night when the rats roamed. But, there was some good news with the new place. The school was right across the street, and there were new kids right downstairs.

I was five years old and anxious to start kindergarten. Going to school was something to do, and it was where the others kids were. And from what Carl told me, it was going to be a lot fun. I could hardly wait.

The classroom was loud and filled with a lot of kids I didn't know. My teacher, Ms. McGinnis, was a tall, heavy, white woman with long hair parted down the middle. Before I started kindergarten, I learned to write and spell my name, but there was a problem. I had learned Beth's last name. Ms. McGinnis tried to correct me, but that was the name I was taught. She requested a Parent/Teacher conference with Beth.

"Shashanna seems to think that her last name is Thomas, and I want to know why she doesn't know her last name."

I remember Beth taking pride in me wanting her last name, but she had to tell me that we weren't related, and that she was my State appointed guardian. I could tell what she was saying was big news, but it would be a while before I understood.

I felt confused and worried because I thought that Beth was going to whip me after the conference, she didn't. I slowly started writing my first name followed by Wilson. It was a hard transition, but I got used to it.

That was the beginning of my discovery of self-identity, and I would soon understand that I was a foster child who was a ward of the State in the custody of DCFS.

I thought of those commercials at night about kids needing food and shelter; they were labeled foster kids. I worried about the other kids at school knowing that I was a foster child. Since I found out via school, why couldn't they? The only thing that made me happy was going to school and making new friends, and I didn't want anything to mess that up. School was becoming real important to me because it got me away from home, which meant away from rats, roaches, Beth, and whippings. My home life wasn't all bad; Granma did tell stories.

Granma told us many stories about "hootenannies" and living Down South. She told me that when she was a little girl in the South, a man had rubbed her head lightly on the sides and kept his hands in the middle of her head; that was the reason she was baldheaded. She told hundreds of these stories, and I believed them all. One story she told affected the way I felt about my mother.

"Shashanna and Carl stayed alone in da attic wit' dogs until me and Beth got dem out of there. We brought dem home, and Shanna's hair had dog shit in there, so we washed huh hair in soap powder."

Granma told that story so many times that I started to picture it, even though I didn't remember it. I recalled my mother being very clean with us, and we were never around any dogs.

I noticed that Carl was never around when Granma told that story, so I felt compelled to ask him, "Did we eva' sleep wit' dogs?"

"Hell naw, who told you dat?" Carl asked in anger.

"Granma."

"She just lyin' to make herself look good."

"Huh?"

"Grown people do that sometimes. It's stupid."

I was relieved to know the truth because the memories of my mother were fading from my mind, and I wanted to keep the ones I had intact. Beth was a mean ass woman, and I still hated her ass, but somehow I came to the conclusion that I wouldn't see my mother again, and that Beth was my new mom.

She used to whip me and Carl so much that we made a game out of the whippings. I had stayed out a few minutes past the street lights coming on, and I was expecting a whipping, but it didn't come until the next morning. I was confused and shocked out of my sleep.

"I told you not to stay yo' ass out afta' the street lights went out! Didn't I tell you?" Beth screamed while striking me with the extension cord.

I couldn't answer because the pain overwhelmed me.

Carl ran in the room and yelled, "Saprise! Saprise! Saprise!"

I cried harder while Carl and Beth laughed. The next day, Carl got a whipping for something he wasn't supposed to do, and I took the liberty to get even.

"Saprise! Saprise! Saprise!"

"Shashanna, Shut up! That's not funny!" Carl said with angry tears.

"You made fun of huh yesterday, so you be quiet!" Beth said to Carl.

Carl used to get hit with sticks, extension cords, shoes, and anything else Beth could get her hands on. After his whipping, Carl beat me up for making fun of him. I didn't always like my brother, and I grew afraid of him, but I still loved him.

As a child, I was plagued with fits; Beth and Granma called them temper tantrums. Every time I got a whipping or couldn't have my way, I would fall out on the floor and then bang my head against the wall as hard as I could, and no one stopped me. One time, I banged my head so hard against the wall that the thick wall plaster cracked.

Beth used to cheer me on and bring people around to witness my episodes.

"Go head and kill yo' self, I don't care, do y'all care?" She would tease while laughing with her friends.

I wasn't having much fun at home, but I did have a best friend, Crystal.

Crystal and I were the same age, she stayed on my block, and we had a lot in common: we were in the same grade, each had one brother, and both loved jumping rope. However, our differences were extreme; Crystal had very short hair, and I had very long hair.

Kids can be cruel. Crystal's hair was very short, and they focused on it calling her, "Crystal Beanie Baldhead Genie," and so did I. Every time she made me mad, I would call her by that name, and it hurt her feelings, but we would argue and make up minutes later. Crystal and I did everything together; we were stuck like glue.

When people saw me, they saw Crystal. I even tried to grow her hair with products we found in the medicine cabinet. A tube of Ambi skin care cream was left in the cabinet, and I thought it was for hair, so I used it on Crystal's hair, and her hair started to grow. It got long enough to braid and put in click-clack balls.

Every summer, Crystal would leave and come back when school started. I was lonely during those summers. One summer, Crystal went away and never came back, and I never found out why.

Exploring Something New

Beth had a lot of boyfriends, but we spent some weekends with the one I remember. His name was Walter. He was fat, white, and eventually I found out he was bald.

One day I was in the bed with Beth and Walter because Carl was sleeping wild on the couch. I did a double take when Walter's baldhead popped out from under the covers. The hair that was usually on Walter's head was on the nightstand.

Totally discombobulated, I asked, "Why is yo' hair ova' there?"

The question wasn't all the way out of my mouth before Beth slapped me, and I didn't ask another hair question.

Beth was wearing a green baby doll gown, and I saw Walter's naked pink ass when I pulled the covers back. I wasn't scared, I was curious because I had never seen a pink ass. I was truly an innocent child.

Beth pulled the top of her gown down, exposing her breast and told me to play with them while Walter watched. I didn't know what she meant by play with them, so I did nothing.

"Put ya hands on these, stupid, and move them around." She ordered.

I played with them, and Walter must have enjoyed it a lot because I had to do this every time we spent the night over his house. At the tender age of seven, I knew touching a grown woman's breast wasn't appropriate, but I felt I was getting closer to Beth, and maybe she would not beat me anymore. But that didn't happen, the whippings kept coming, but we did stop going over Walter's house.

With Crystal gone, I made a new friend, Reggie. He lived next door to us, and he had lots of toys, and there was plenty to eat at his house. Reggie was a chubby, fair-skinned boy with fat cheeks. Reggie's whole family was obese, and his mother cooked delicious dinners. She would feed me every time I was at their house, and I loved it. I did not leave their house until dinner was over.

One day, I had on some clear plastic shoes, and when I took them off Reggie's mother stared at my feet. She lifted them up and saw the blisters on my soles.

"Shanna, what happen to yo' foots, did Beth do dat?" Reggie's mother asked with her hands on her oversized hips.

I did not answer Reggie's mother because I knew that I would get in trouble. I used to get beatings on parts of my body that got me into trouble. For example, if I stole something, I would get beat on my hands. I got blisters on my feet because I was running through the house. Beth had thrown hot water hot on my feet, and she beat them with an extension cord.

Reggie's mother pulled me by my arm to my house. She confronted Beth, and they argued about the blisters on my feet. Beth got livid and made up a story about what happened. She told me I wasn't allowed to go over to Reggie's house.

I didn't listen because I enjoyed the decent meals, and Beth wasn't stopping me from eating them. I used to sneak over to Reggie's house when Beth went to work.

Reggie's family used to save pop bottles for me, so I could cash them in at the corner store. I would get all of the boxes of candies that the store had: Alexander the Grape, Lemonheads, Red Hots, and Boston Baked Beans. After I ate the candy, I would blow in the empty boxes and make instruments out of them.

I figured more people than Reggie's family had empty pop bottles, so I started hustling bottles. I went from door-to-door asking people for their pop empty bottles; sometimes I had to run errands for them, but most times they just gave them to me.

My appearance was like a homeless child, so I guess most of the adults felt sorry for me. My clothes were dirty, and so was my skin. I remember taking baths in washing powder and calling it my bubble bath. It caused my skin to itch like crazy, which made me take less "bubble baths."

Granma would wash our clothes with her hands every Saturday in the tub. We never went to the Laundromat. But, Granma developed arthritis in her hands and wasn't able to wash our clothes any longer, which meant I had to wash my own clothes starting at six years old. Granma taught me how to wash clothes the best she could, and I hated grinding my knuckles together because my skin would come off. I even washed my hair with the washing powder.

    Not being the cleanest child meant I endured harsh criticism from the kids at school. I liked school anyway, but to defend myself from the insults, I got into fights, but fighting didn't stop the insults; the kids had too much ammunition. They talked about me being dirty but still smelling like washing powder, and they teased me about looking different. My skin was lighter than everyone else's, and my hair was longer than any other girl, which meant I was called: honky, white ass, white girl, and Puerto Rican.

    I tried so hard to look like everybody around me and prove that I was black. I put a hot comb in my hair and damn near set it on fire. I couldn't change my hair or my skin color. But, one day I went to my "aunt", Beth's sister's, house to spend the weekend and got help.

    Beth's sister gave all the girls baths, and that night I was the last to go. She ran my water and put actual bubble bath in the running water. I was in awe. I got in the tub and was amazed by the silky feel of it. Later, Beth's sister came in with the towels.

    "Shanna, Look at yo' skin! It look like you been rolling in mud, and it dried on you! What my susta be doing wit' you, uh, uh, uh?" Beth's sister said with her arms folded together.

    Beth's sister took the towel and the soap and started washing me, which made me feel very uncomfortable, but I let her continue.

    "You wash dis way. You lookin' at me?" Beth's sister said with a stern voice.

    "Yea," I whispered.

Beth's sister washed me hard, not so hard that it hurt me, but she washed hard enough to clean my skin. I felt a big difference. After I got out of that tub, the water was muddy, but I felt brand new, and I slept like a baby.

After that weekend with Beth's sister, I started taking my clothes over to Reggie's house to get washed because I got tired of sore knuckles and half clean clothes, but Beth caught me.

"What you doing wit that bag of clothes?"

"I'm going next door' so Reggie's momma can wash my clothes."

"You ain't going nowhere with the clothes I bought you! Put that shit down!" Beth said while snatching the bag of clothes from my grasp.

So, I waited until Beth went to work and got my clothes clean, and they smelled like fabric softener... fresh. I couldn't change my skin or my hair, but I could smell and look better.

Gotta Go To Church, Now

I had to go to church every Sunday for a while because Beth was in love with the Pastor. So she forced Carl and me to go to church with her. I remember her wearing a tight ass black sweater dress, and I remember her buying new shoes and outfits for church while she shopped at the Goodwill for our church clothes.

She would make the Goodwill clothes sound special, "Shanna, girl, that coat I got you is a Pointer Susta coat," and I believed that crap, so I looked forward to wearing my Goodwill Sunday best.

Carl got into a fight at church and embarrassed Beth, so she stopped making him go, and that left me and her. Eventually, I started looking forward to church because I had made friends there, and the money Beth gave me for the collection plate went to the corner store for penny candy.

Easter Sunday was the best because this was the only time I got new clothes: a dress and accessories, along with an Easter basket. On one particular Easter I had a speech to memorize. Beth promised that if I didn't learn the speech she would whip my ass, so I memorized the speech, and when Easter arrived I was ready, but the program was canceled.

Easter, Easter everywhere all over the sea, when it's time for Easter eggs please stop for me.

Reverend Mac, the preacher Beth loved, had a Cadillac, but the church didn't have doorknobs or locks on the bathroom stalls, and most of us walked or caught the bus to church. But, what confused me more was the Holy Ghost.

I was scared as hell when women had the Holy Ghost. I was afraid of the hollering, and the falling on the floor with their dresses up over their heads, and they always caught the Holy Ghost in front of the preacher, and I never saw a man catch the Holy Ghost.

Beth explained that when the spirit hits a person they have no control over it. I wondered why a "Holy" spirit would have someone to throw themselves on the floor. I didn't believe Beth's explanation. I began watching people for myself and decided some were faking, but some really got the gift of the Holy Spirit from God, and that kind of scared me. I was worried that the Holy Ghost would hit me, but I soon learned it wasn't the Holy Ghost I had to watch out for.

Girls at the church started calling me honky and pulling my hair. At first church was different than school, but it didn't last long. I couldn't escape the ignorance and the curiosity of my appearance. Girls who had been friendly quickly turned on me and started calling me white girl. I didn't want to fight at church, but I would have.

Lance, my childhood abuser, was in the Inspirational Choir. And all men in the choir acted like girls, including Lance. Beth said they were all "sissies." I didn't know what a sissy was, but the choir became the best part of church for me. The choir director switched his touché from side to side, and the others played the tambourines and washboards. The washboard, along with a spoon, made an instrument that thrilled the church. Lance and his crew made the choir sound good.

Later, Lance and his friends were removed from the choir because they were gay and eventually removed from the church. The church choir became dull and was never be the same. Eventually, I lost interest in going to church, and Beth gave up arguing with me every Sunday.

The Effects of Home Scars

I was no stranger to ass whippings, and since I was getting older and more defiant, my whippings increased from every once in a while to two or three times a week. My child neighbors used to go in the gangway and listen to me yell and scream then they would wait until I came outside and make fun of me.

"Ahh haa! You got that weekly ass whuppin'! Damn! Don't yo' ass get tired of getting beat?"

"That wasn't me, that was Carl," I would say while pointing upstairs.

"We ain't stupid, it was yo' ass getting tow up!"

"Leave me alone!"

Every time I got a whipping, I'd wear long sleeved shirts and pants to hide the welts on my skin.

My personal appearance still wasn't up to par, but it had gotten better because I washed my own clothes, and I learned how to French braid my hair. The girl who made the fun of my clothes the most was my new friend Brenda.

"You had on that same thang yesterday, is you po'?" She'd ask this in front of the other kids on the block.

"Naw, I aint po'!"

I teased Brenda a lot about her failing fourth grade and not being in fifth like me, but I had done it so much that it was poor ammunition against her teasing me about my clothes.

"I heard y'all go to the Goodwill to buy clothes. My momma carry me to the mall and buy me good clothes."

Brenda made me aware of name brand clothes like Sergio Valente, Polo shirts, and Gloria Vanderbilt jeans. I never saw Brenda in name brand clothes, but she'd brag about them because her sisters and cousins had them.

I was really bothered by the constant insults about my attire, but I never told anyone. Beth and Granma were constantly telling Carl and me how they rescued us from dirt, and we were very fortunate to have what we had: clothes on our backs, and a roof over our heads.

My grades were poor, and I started fighting all the time because of the teasing. I found myself having to defend myself more, and fighting became the norm.

My home situation effected my school action as well. Some mornings, I would fall asleep on my desk because I slept with Granma's loud snoring ass, and I couldn't sleep. The teacher gave me assignments that seemed so hard that I gave up on doing class work, but I did have good attendance, and that helped some. I was given homework, but I never brought it home. After school, I just went outside to play. No one was concerned about my education.

I began to hate school, not only my classmates made fun of me, but my teacher, Mrs. Mason, did as well. She would tell me over and over in front of the class that I was going to fail her class because I was dumb, and she wished she had a Dunce hat to sit me in the corner with. The whole class would laugh and laugh. I acted like I wasn't bothered, but I was.

I caught Chicken Pox and missed the IOWA test, which meant that I had to take the test later. When I returned to school, Mrs. Mason quickly approached me.

"Shashanna, here is a booklet and a number two pencil and a sheet numbered from one to a hundred. This booklet is Reading and Comprehension. Each question is multiple-choice, and you'll indicate your answer on the card, A, B, C, or D. Fill in the circle completely so the machine will read your answer. I will time you for each subject, and you'll get a break in between subjects. Do you have any questions?"

"No," I said with confusion.

"You may begin."

I felt troubled and impatient with the materials that were in front of me. I thought that daydreaming would be more interesting. So, I daydreamed. When I snapped out of the daydream, I realized that I was taking a test, so I hurried and filled in the circles quickly. I took the test up to Mrs. Mason's desk. Mrs. Mason looked at me with amazement.

"Are you finished with your test already?" Mrs. Mason asked with her eyebrows raised.

"Yeah, Mrs. Mason." I said nonchalantly.

Mrs. Mason looked at me and said that she hoped that I got the correct answers on my test because if I didn't, I would be in her class again next year. I ignored Mrs. Mason and proceeded to guess the answers on the entire week long test. I continued fifth grade without concern about what was going to happen to me or not happen.

I used to look for Brenda at school, but I never saw her because she was in a lower grade, and their lunch schedule was different from ours, so I only saw her on the block. I used to look down on Brenda for not being in the fifth grade, until "that" day came.

Everyone in my classroom received their IOWA test scores on an orange card. I looked at mine and didn't know what my scores meant, so this boy named Juan asked to see my scores. He had an, "I know you failed," look on his face, but at that time I didn't care. Juan looked at my scores then he showed this other boy named Keith, and suddenly my scores made it around the room.

"OOOOOOOOO! You have some real low scores, you gonna be in the fifth grade again." Juan said loudly.

I guess Mrs. Mason heard the commotion and came over to my desk.

"Let me see your scores." She asked, holding her glasses down.

I gave the orange card to Mrs. Mason, and she looked at me and shook her head.

"I told you, you should've taken your time on the test, didn't I? You took the test too quickly, and now you are going to be in my class again while everyone moves on to the sixth-grade." Mrs. Mason said sternly. I thought to myself, *Yeah right!* "Shashanna, I don't think you get it. Your scores are 2.3 and less, which means your level of learning is less than a third grade student." Mrs. Mason said while shaking her glasses in her right hand.

I still didn't really get it. I was looking forward to summer vacation more than worrying about my failing grades. When I got home, no one asked me about my grades, as a matter of fact, no one asked about my report card because nobody cared, so why should I. It was funny that I got beatings for breathing too hard, but my failing grades were waived.

My only real problem was facing Brenda. I had made fun of her all year about her being held back. Before I could get my front door open, Brenda was shoving her report card in my face.

"What room is you gonna be in next year," she asked with excitement.

I frowned and said, "I hate school."

"What happened Shanna?" Brenda asked with a smirk on her face.

"I think I failed." I said in a low voice

"Girl, we probably be in the same room!" Brenda said as if failing was normal.

CHAPTER 5

Summer Madness

In spite of me failing the fifth grade, summer break had finally come, and I was going to make the most of each day. As the weather got warmer, the kids on the block started coming out to play and sit on their porches. That summer was different because the boys on the block started noticing me and making comments.

"Shanna, yo' breast got big ova' the winta! Damn!" D'Angello said while holding his crotch.

Apparently, I had a flat chest the last time those nasty boys saw me. Brenda used to make fun of my flat chest and would compare them to hers; hers were bigger. I didn't like attention to my girly parts because I was a tomboy who didn't understand why my breasts were sore. I hated going to the store with Beth to buy bras because she'd embarrass me to the utmost.

"Shanna, you skipped the training bra and went straight to the women bras! Let me see what size you is." Beth said with extreme ghetto fabulousness.

Beth was so loud that everyone in the bra store looked at the both of us while I looked down with embarrassment. In my head, I was thinking; *Lord, please get me up out of here.* I totally ignored the fact that I had become different to everyone, including the boys I played sports with.

One day, I went to the park to see what was going on, a few guys on the block were playing football and I wanted in.

"Can I play wit' y'all?" I asked.

"You sure you want to play this game, girl?" A boy with a brick shaped head asked.

"I played befo'." I said while getting closer.

"Okaaaay!" The brick head boy said, as if I didn't know what I was about to get myself into.

I got in position to catch the football and caught it. I ran towards the goal, and all of a sudden, this big boy named Jacoby tackled me and squeezed my breast until I cried. I never attempted to play football again.

But, I continued to play basketball. We played in the alley with a bicycle rim nailed to the telephone pole. That was the neighborhood b-ball court, and both boys and girls played there.

I started making friends with girls from all over the neighborhood, and they found out that I jumped double-dutch like no one's business. I used to jump rope so long that my side would start to hurt, and the girls who were turning the rope would pant with impatience.

A girl named Nona jumped as good as me, and we became partners. We were so good that we filled out a card for the McDonald's Double-Dutch contest, but we never heard from anyone. While other kids were riding their bikes and skating, I climbed trees and played sports because I didn't own a bike, skates, or skateboard. All I could do was watch or ask the kids who owned bikes or skates to use theirs.

I became painfully aware that I had less than other kids; it was a stressful realization. Add to that my physical appearance changing, and I was a mess. With no one to explain the changes, I relied on my ten year old mind to figure things out. Trial and error were my teachers.

Not only did my breasts start to grow, but I soon discovered my menstrual. Surprisingly, I wasn't terrified to see my cycle because Beth used to leave her tampons in the bathroom in the seat of her panties. She left her underwear exposed so many times that I had to ask.

"Why you bleed in yo' panties?"

Beth explained the best her ignorant self could.

"Women comes on their periods every month, and you will too."

So, I was informed about my menstrual cycle, but no one told me about the painful cramps that would come along with it.

I was in Schaumburg, Illinois over at my cousin's house. We went to see Richard Pryor's movie, "The Toy," and all of a sudden, I was attacked by cramps so severe I couldn't watch the movie. Later that night, I was watching television and saw a Pamprin commercial that informed of menstrual cramps.

When I got home, things got worse. Not a week later, I woke up in Cook County Hospital with Beth and Carl looking down at me.

"Shanna, you okay baby?" Beth asked.

I knew something was wrong because Beth had never called me baby.

"Shanna, can you hear me? You fell out", Carl said with his eyes open wide.

I couldn't remember anything prior to waking up. I was still sort of out of it and didn't say anything.

"Shanna, you started shakin' and foaming at tha mouth. I 'm waiting on tha docta to tell me what happen." Beth said while rubbing my arm.

Beth was worried, and that terrified me. My tongue and mouth were sore, and dried blood was on my shirt. I was in the hall of a hospital on a stretcher. We waited like forever and then the doctor finally came out to look at me. He had me follow a light he held in his hand.

Then he snapped a capsule under my nose and told me to, "Inhale deeply."

I smelled ammonia. He looked at me like he had something real bad to tell me. He shook his head then he pulled Beth away from me, and they started talking. I looked down at the dried blood and the frantic expression on Carl's face and I got scared.

Beth came back to me, "Shanna, you had a seizure, and tha doctor said you have to take medicine now. OK?"

A seizure, that didn't sound so bad. I had to gargle with this concoction that the doctor gave me to rinse the blood out of my mouth, and they let me go home.

When we got home, everyone was nice to me and waited on me hand and foot. I liked the attention and played it out. We had to go to the doctor's office the next day. He told me I had Epilepsy. I immediately thought I was going to die. The name sounded so horrible, Epilepsy.

"Beth, am I gonna die?"

Beth laughed before she answered my inquiry.

"No, you jus' have to take medicine, you OK. You hurt herself havin' temper tantrums, and beating ya head against all those walls. Ya got nerve damage in your brain."

That didn't sound as bad as dying. I continued to receive special treatment at home, but I couldn't go outside for a few days, so I stayed in bed. At the age of eleven, I knew nothing about the side effects of medicine. All I knew was I slept better with no disturbance from Granma's snoring. For some reason, I started to think about my mother and wondered where she was and how she was doing, but my image of my mom was never a clear one. I had been away from my mother for more than five years.

Soon after my discovered Epilepsy, I was allowed to go outside and play with my friends. Things were back to normal. Every now and then, Carl would do something mean to me: hit me in my thigh or dig in his butt and wipe his finger across my nose. I damn near hated him, but my hatred wouldn't last long.

Carl was sick with a cold, and he had a pickle in the refrigerator. I ate it. When he stumbled to the refrigerator to get it, he saw it was gone.

"Who ate my pickle?"

I yelled back, "I did!"

"You know I'm sick, and that pickle wasn't yours," Carl said in his nasal voice.

"I'm sorry," I said.

Carl got a broom and started hitting me with it, so I ran, but he followed me and continued to beat me. I must have had a seizure because I woke up in the bathroom covered in blood.

"Come on Shanna, come on, I'm sorry, I'm sorry," Carl was trying to wake me up.

I saw the worry in my brother's eyes, and I hugged him to assure him that I was okay.

When Beth got home, she was drunk, which didn't happen much, but she noticed that I was hurt and asked Carl what happened to me.

"She fell on da bafroom flo' and had anotha seizure." Carl lied.

"Uh uh, he hit me becuz I ate his pickle, and I fell out."

Beth got mad and cursed Carl out, but she didn't whip him.

I enjoyed the rest of my summer with my friends. No one outside of our family knew about my illness. What happened in our house was supposed to stay in the house, but in our house we never talked about stuff pertaining to personal matters or feelings. We just existed.

CHAPTER 6

Fed Up!

Carl dropped out of school and didn't go back when school started that fall. He was spending nights away from home, and nobody seemed to care but me.

When he did come home after being gone for days, Granma or Beth would not say a word to him. It was like Carl was grown, and I was still a little kid who Beth could whip.

When I came home after the first day of school Carl was there, and I was happy to see him, but a plate or something was left in the sink from the night before, and Beth was snapping. That day at school hadn't gone well either; even though I had gone to summer school the school administration wanted me to transfer to an alternative school. I was trying to talk to Carl about the alternative school, since he went there too, but Beth wouldn't let us talk. She kept screaming about the plate.

I had just walked in, and Beth was calling me into the kitchen with anger in her voice, but Beth was always angry. I went in the kitchen to see what she wanted.

"You didn't wash all tha dishes like I asked you!" Beth yelled while putting her cigarette out.

I told her that I had washed the dishes and checked the sink.

"Somebody put that plate in tha sink afta I wash tha dishes already."

"Bitch, you lying, and tha truth ain't in ya!"

That was Beth's favorite line.

"No I ain't. I washed all the dishes."

"Bitch, ya don't go word for word with me!"

I knew it was coming, and when the slap arrived I saw lightening.

"I hate you!" Beth stood still, looking at me like she didn't know me. I hated her ass. "I hate you!" I screamed again.

Beth walked quickly to her room and came back with an extension cord. I made up my mind right then; Beth wasn't whipping anymore.

She slapped her hand with the cord, "I'ma tear yo' ass up!"

I was looking for a way past her without getting hit by that cord. Beth charged me, swinging the extension cord. Without thinking, I grabbed the cord, wrapping my hand in it.

"Let the cord go, bitch!" Beth said with shock on her face.

Carl came into the kitchen and grabbed Beth and pushed her against this door that lead downstairs to the first floor apartment. We kept pushing Beth against the door until she went through it. Carl and I fell on top of her.

"You gonna leave my susta alone."

"Get the fuck up off me, mutha fucka!" Beth said while struggling to get up.

"Not until you tell me you gonna leave my susta alone!"

"I'ma call tha police!" Granma yelled in panic from the doorway.

"You shoulda been calling tha police when this bitch first started whupping us with cords!" Carl yelled at Granma.

"Carl, get off her cuz I don't want you to be in jail," Granma said to Carl.

Carl got off of Beth, and she went to her room, defeated.

Carl left right after her, and it was long time before I saw him again. I began to understand that Carl was not a kid. Beth and Granma treated him different, and he was different. Beth knew she couldn't whip him anymore, and after that day, she knew whipping me was over too.

When I went back to school, they transferred me to the alternative school. I knew kids there with major problems, but the only thing wrong with me was bad grades, or so I thought. When I walked in the school, kids were hanging out in the halls. I was leery about going to the "Bad School," but I had to if I wanted to stay in school. Carl dropping out kind of scared me.

Going to school wasn't great, but it was better than staying home with angry Beth and Granma. I was not exactly sure how, but I knew school could make life better, and I knew Carl had lost that chance.

At the alternative school, I was placed in a class where the kids fought every day. The teacher was obviously afraid of the students, which made me afraid, and having a light complexion made me an instant target. From day one, I had to call on everything I knew about fighting.

Before the teacher could introduce me, I was asked, "What's yo' name, girl?" by this girl dressed like a boy.

"Shanna," I said while looking her up and down.

"Why you here?" The boyish looking girl asked.

"Because I got into a lot of fights," it seemed like a good answer at the time.

"Awwwh, so you be fighting, we gone see."

I just took a seat because the teacher did not direct me to one.

"Shanna, what you doing here?"

I looked behind me, and it was my brother's girlfriend's niece, Sandy, who I didn't like because of her nasty attitude. I wanted to ignore her greeting.

"I didn't know you went here, Shanna," Sandy said as if we got along.

"I jus' started going here. How long you been going here?" I asked.

"I been going here since last year. I hate it here. These girls always trying to beat me up."

"Yea, I can see what you talking about, but I will kick they ass if they step to me." I said it loud enough for Sandy and anyone else that was listening to hear.

A couple of heads turned towards me, and I stared them down in return.

After class, I went to the girl's restroom, and these girls confronted me about what I said to Sandy.

"Oh, you gonna kick our ass, huh?" The boyish looking girl said while getting in my face.

"Fo' what!" I said with a frown.

"You tha one wanna kick our ass!" She said while poking my head with her finger.

I slapped her finger off of my face and stepped to her.

"What chu gonna do?" She said while her hommies blocked the girl's restroom.

"Fuck it, I don't care, we can go right now, all of y'all!"

I dropped my book bag to the floor and pushed her hard, and that's when the fight broke out.

Yeah, I got my butt whipped, but they took some hard knocks too. One of them had a bloody nose when it was over. I had bruises on my cheeks but lost no blood. I kneed the boyish girl so hard in the stomach that she was still on the floor when the fight was over; I learned that from playing with the boys.

When boys fought, they always looked each other in the eye. I'd learned to look the enemy straight in the eyes and get at least one good lick in. My rep was established the first day at the "bad" school. I defended myself.

Kids wanted to talk about what had happened, but I didn't because I wanted to focus on my class assignments and getting up out of that school. I wanted to go back to a regular school. But I had no idea how much my life was about to change.

It started at Beth's house with a visit from my "real" grandmother.

Over the years, she would pop up every now and then and make an appearance, but this time was different; our unknown grandfather had died, and we had to go to the funeral. Carl and I looked at each other as if to say, who said we had to go to a stranger's funeral? Grandmother left Carl her contact information to give us a chance to think about the situation.

We were both curious about how our family was doing and decided to go.

The day of the funeral, I was anxious about seeing my mother. I didn't want to be bitter towards her, but I was still very angry with her and my grandmother.

I had on a lavender dress with a flower stitched to the upper left side. I was looking cute. I remember arriving at the mega church with strangers who happened to be my family. My brother and I were stared at when we arrived, as if we were stars or outcasts.

When Carl and I were seated our mother was already there. She turned and looked at us and started to cry. Carl was more receptive than me because I hated Momma for what she'd done and what we had to endure. All through the funeral, I felt like a visitor or an outsider. I was a foster child, a ward of the State of Illinois, and I was in a church filled with my family, wasn't shit right about that. These were the people that were supposed to take of me and Carl; our family.

My mother just stared at Carl and me during most of the service while mourning her father's death. After the formal funeral, I was ready to go, but I had to play this "family" event out.

We were in the crowed lobby of the funeral home smiling at strangers when I heard, "Shashanna!"

I looked, and it was my mom, trying to get to me.

"I'm ova here." I said.

She pushed through people to get to us.

"I'm so glad to see you. How have you been?" She hugged me with tears in her eyes.

"I been fine," I said nonchalantly.

Then my mother reached to touch my face, but I jerked away and stepped out of her embrace. By the hurt look that appeared on her face, I guess my moving away upset her.

I had to ask, "Why did you leave us?" My voice was filled with fury.

Carl shook his head yeah, like he wanted to ask the same question.

"Shanna not here." Mother whispered.

"Yeah, I wanna know too," Carl said with more volume in his voice.

"Beth took y'all from me, I wanna kill that bitch." My mother answered with tears pouring down her face.

I didn't believe her. People couldn't just take kids. I knew that much. She was looking at me like she was begging me to believe her.

Then she asked, "What is that mark on your face?"

"What mark?" I said while holding my face.

I totally forgot the fight at school and Beth hitting me with the extension cord; hell, the mark could have come from either place, and I probably had more than one mark. And why the hell was she asking?

"It looks like a hand print or something, Beth hit you?" Mother said with anger.

I looked down, wanting to ask her when, which time, but at the same time, I didn't want to say shit to my mother. She didn't care about me getting hit. She didn't care about me or Carl. I wanted to go.

"Yeah, dat bitch hit you. I hate huh for takin' my kids!" Mother said and started to cry…again.

I looked at my mother wondering why she was concerned about my wellbeing, that shit was phony, she was phony, so I said, "You had years to find out about us if you wanted to know."

"Yeah," Carl said, sounding as angry as me.

I turned from her and saw my grandmother who brought us to the funeral.

"Granma, I'm ready to go!" I was almost yelling.

"Okay, I'm gonna let everybody know we leaving."

"Now!" Carl said, and he did yell.

When we got home, Beth tried to coax Carl and me into telling her what happened at the funeral. I didn't want to talk to her or anyone else. I was mad at the world. But once Beth offered money to hear about the funeral, Carl opened up and told her about seeing cousins and Mama. Carl taking Beth's money and telling her everything that happened made me mad at him too.

"Fuck all y'all," I said under my breath and went to bed.

I started going over to my real grandmother's house every weekend to get to know her, and to get away from Beth's house. My grandmother lived alone in an apartment, and it was so clean and organized that I thought that she was rich. She showed me pictures of when I was an infant, which I found amazing because I always wondered how I looked as a baby.

"Grandma, how old was I?"

"Right here, you three months. This is Carl when he was a baby." Grandmother said while turning the pages to the family's photo album.

I never asked my grandmother why she didn't keep me and Carl, I wanted to, but I didn't because I wanted to keep going over to her apartment. It made me feel good to be around her. She was clean and my real family. Beth was nasty and my foster home.

Things got better with me visiting my grandmother. I started doing well again in school, and I was getting to know my real people. One day, a lady stopped by the house asking for Beth, but she wasn't home. The lady proceeded to ask questions about Beth and myself. I felt strange talking to this woman, but for some reason I felt that I needed to answer her questions.

"Are you Shashanna?"
"Yea!"
"I'm a social worker from DCFS."
"DC who?"
"Did Ms. Taylor ever hit you?"
"Why?"
"I was told that you were being abused by…Beth."
"Yes, she hit me."
"How long has she been striking you?"
"I don't know."
"Did she recently hit you in your face?"

Just then I knew what was going on, and I knew my mother had called this lady and told her about the hand print on my face. I looked at the lady and told her I was through answering questions and that she had to leave. She said that she'd be back again and left her contact information on a card. Later, I told Beth that a lady came by the house, and she wanted to see her.

"What damn lady?" Beth asked ignorantly.

"I don't know, but she left a number," I said, giving Beth the card.

The next week the same lady visited Beth, but my presence wasn't needed. I was in suspense and waited patiently until the lady left the house.

"Shanna, you told that worker I hit you?" Beth yelled.

"Yeah," I said with courage.

"See, now they gone take you away, and you won't see Carl or me again." Beth said wickedly. I instantly became worried and began to cry. "Ain't no need fo' cryin' na! Tell them that you lied, and you didn't know wut you was talking 'bout." Beth suggested.

"Ok, I will." I said in relief.

Even Carl told me to tell the lady that I lied, so we wouldn't separate. When the lady came, she wanted to talk to me, and I explained that Beth never hit me and I lied because I was mad at her. The lady was writing on a piece of paper and looking at me if I wasn't telling the truth.

"Am I going to be taken away from my brotha?" I asked.

"No," The lady said, and assured me that I wasn't going anywhere, and Carl and I would remain together.

A few weeks later, Beth took me to her room with this serious look on her face.

"You have to pack yo' clothes because you is leaving tomorrow!" Beth said nonchalantly.

"What?"

I thought Beth was lying because I told on her, but she wasn't.

"See, that's what you get for lyin' to them, telling them I slap you."

"You did slap me I said."

"Now yo' ass is gonna have to go, and yo' ain't gonna see Carl anymo'."

I started to cry, but I was still in denial, so I didn't pack my clothes. Beth got garbage bags and packed my clothes.

"You should have kept yo' mouf close, and you won't be leaving here."

The next day Grandma told me I had to stay home from school, and the lady was coming to pick me up.

"Did Beth go to work?" I asked.

"Yeah, she at work."

All I saw was garbage bags full of clothes waiting in the long hall. No one was home but Grandma and me, which made me wonder if anyone cared or was this cruel joke.

"What time do this lady supposed to come?" I asked.

"Ten o'clock." Grandma said.

"Okay," I said, as if everything was a hoax.

Ten o'clock on the dot, the lady came for me. I felt sad about leaving Carl, but what I didn't understand was why he wasn't there with me. I left in a horrible state of mind wondering about where I was going and when I was going to see my brother again.

CHAPTER 7

Me, Without Carl

Carl and I were no longer together, but I still had a mustard seed of hope that my leaving was a mistake. During the ride to my destination, the worker asked if I wanted anything to eat. I had no desire to eat.

"No. How long before we get there?"

I had never been on a ride that lasted as long as that one. My patience had grown short with worrying about my brother.

When we finally made to the house, I wanted to throw up from worry. The door opened before we knocked or rang a bell. I was introduced to the lady of the house as we sat on her couch.

"Shashanna, this is your new foster mother, Ms. Hanks. This is Shashanna."

Ms. Hanks was hard looking woman due to her short jerry curl, buckeyes, and being built like a man.

"You gonna like it here," the social worker said with a smile.

"Just relax and make yo'self at home." Ms. Hanks exclaimed.

Ms. Hanks and the worker filed out paperwork for what seemed like forever. I didn't like the place because I was away from the people I knew. Ms. Hanks and the worker took me on a tour of the house and showed me where I was going to sleep. In the room, there was a set of bunk beds and a single twin bed next to it. Apparently, there were other kids living there, but it was a school day, so they must have been in school.

"Shashanna, you are in a better place, and I'll visit as soon as you settled in." The worker said with confidence. "Ms. Hanks, it's been a pleasure to meet you, Shanna take care." The social worker said before she left.

I watched the worker as she walked out and drove away. Tears welded up in my eyes because reality had set in. When the worker left, Ms. Hanks started telling me the names of the other girls who lived in the household, and she told me her house rules. One of the rules was we couldn't come through the front door because Ms. Hanks wanted to keep her carpet clean.

"I have one daughter of my own, two foster girls, and you will be the third. Lenzy is my "real" daughter's name and the other two fosta' girls' names are Ingrid and Nancy." Ms. Hanks said with her buckeyes on me.

I wanted to go back home, but I kept quiet and pretended that I was listening to her.

"Oh, you want somethin' to eat… what's yo' name again?" Ms. Hanks asked.

"Shashanna," I said quietly.

"Shashanna, you want something to eat?" Ms. Hanks asked again.

"No," I said sadly.

"Well, let me know when you hongry." Ms. Hanks said then walked away.

I went to the room and lay down and cried myself to sleep. When I woke up, there were three girls sitting around the room.

"Hi, what's your name, new girl?" One girl asked.

"Shashanna," I answered as my voice trembled. I looked around because I forgot that I was in a new place, and sadness set back in. I sat on the bed until I had to use the bathroom. "Where is the bathroom?" I asked.

"Down the hall to yo' right." One of the girls answered.

I looked in the mirror and my eyes were swollen with red rings and I felt exactly how I looked. When I returned to the room, Ms. Hanks' daughter, Lenzy, asked me where I was from, and I told her the west side of Chicago.

"Awww, I heard about that side of town, they bad!" Lenzy said in a derogatory tone.

"Where is this?" I asked.

"This is Chicago Heights!" Lenzy said proudly.

"Chicago what?" I asked with my face scrunched.

"It's a suburb!" Lenzy said.

Lenzy was this short baldhead brat that had a nasty attitude. I could tell from her body language and the way she addressed me. I was thinking, *they probably think they are better than me because they stay live in the suburbs, and I came from the worst part of the Chicago.* From that moment, I didn't say much of anything because I was around strange people in a strange town.

Not knowing how far away I was from Chicago, confirmed that I wouldn't see my brother anytime again, and I cried some more. I began to feel that my situation was my fault because I should've never told on Beth to Mother. I must admit that this house was ten times cleaner than Beth's house, but it wasn't home. I missed my friends and especially Brenda. I wondered how her baby girl was. Later, everyone was called to the kitchen table for dinner, but I was a no show, so Ms. Hanks came to the room to remind me that it was dinner and I can't eat at a later time.

"I'm not hongry!" I said with my face buried in my pillow.

"Okay, suit yo'self," Ms. Hanks said nonchalantly.

Since I was introverted and didn't want to socialize with the other girls, they left me alone and went into other areas in the house. Before I knew it, it was time for bed, and the other girls had to come in the room that I was in and got dressed for bed.

"You don't talk?" One of the girls asked.

"Yeah, I talk." I said.

"What's wrong?" One of the girls asked with concern.

"Nothin'," I said quickly.

"If she don't want to say nothing, leave huh alone."

Before I went to sleep, I asked Ms. Hanks could I call my brother. She told me that she couldn't let me call anyone until the paper work with DCFS was processed. I woke up still mad about that.

"You gon' be alright, ok," the tall girl said.

"Who is you?" I asked.

"Ingrid, and this is my susta, Nancy." Ingrid said.

I waved and put my head back in my pillow and cried myself asleep once again.

The next morning, the girls were up making noise as they got dressed for school. Ms. Hanks offered me breakfast, but I was simply not in the mood for breakfast or talking to her.

"I'm not hungry," I said once again.

"Okay, suit yo'self. I tell you what, I'll leave a plate for you on tha table, and it would be there fuh you."

I was hungry, but I didn't want to be at Ms. Hanks' house, and I wasn't happy. Hunger set in, and I eased into the kitchen and quietly ate what was on the plate. After I ate, I went in the bedroom and went through my clothes. The lavender dress I wore at my Grandfather's funeral reminded me of Carl.

That first morning, Ms. Hanks stayed in her bedroom, and I stayed in mine; we didn't make any attempt to speak to each other, and silence was golden. When the girls got back, I lay down in my bed and turned towards the wall.

"Damn, she still ain't talking to nobody! If she don't want to be here, she should had stayed where she was!" It was Lenzy, Ms. Hanks' daughter.

Lenzy's bullshit made me want to say something, but I didn't because I was still depressed.

"Lenzy, leave that girl alone!" Nancy said.

I heard Nancy's voice for the first time, but it was a condescending tone, as if she was laughing with Lenzy instead of defending me.

Days had passed, and I began to come out of my shell, largely due to hunger. Everyone was at the kitchen table eating, and the way they all looked at me made me want to go back into the room, but I didn't. We ate in silence, but I caught their eyes looking at me, so I didn't finish all of my food.

"You full already?" Ingrid said.

"Yeah," I said.

"I think she don't like what my momma cooked!" Lenzy said.

I didn't comment because a boy was walking into the kitchen through the back door.

"Hi!" He spoke to the table then went down stairs to the basement as quickly as he came in.

"That's my brutha, Ron, you like him don't chu?" Lenzy queried.

I didn't like myself much at that time, never mind a boy, so I didn't answer, but I knew I didn't like Lenzy. After dinner, I returned to my bed. They girls came into the room and started talking about "New Edition" and other meaningless topics.

I rolled from facing the wall to facing them and told them, "I'm tryin' to sleep."

Of course, Lenzy had something to say.

"We can talk all we want to. This is my momma's house. Nobody said anything to yo' white ass anyway!"

"Bitch, I ain't white, and you need to shut yo' ugly ass up befo' I make you!"

Ms. Hanks opened the door and told us to be quiet and to go to sleep.

"Foster girl," Lenzy said in a low tone, but loud enough for me to hear.

"Fuck you," I said.

I really was a foster girl, and Ms. Hanks place made that title real, and my sadness became anger. I was a DCFS Ward of the State, and being a ward and not a daughter pissed me off. I was mad at my mother, Beth, and Carl.

The morning after showers and breakfast, Ingrid and Nancy quietly told me how much they hated Lenzy because she was always bringing up the fact that they were foster kids and she wasn't. I listened to them, but I didn't care about them or Lenzy. My life had been turned upside down. I noticed when Lenzy came out of the bathroom, Ingrid and Nancy quickly dispersed as Lenzy walked toward the bedroom.

"I know y'all ain't talking about me too, huh! Y'all ain't nothing but fosta kids, and if it wasn't fo' my momma, y'all won't have anywhere to stay!" Snipped Lenzy.

"You need to shut yo' ass up," I said.

"Momma, this fosta girl in here talking bad about me," Lenzy whined.

"Don't worry about huh, you hurry up and get dressed fo' school. Speakin' of school, Shashanna, you will start school next week." Ms. Hanks said through the door.

"Good, you'll go to school wit' us, I can't wait!" Ingrid said smiling.

They got dressed and left for school, leaving me alone in the room.

I hated being there, but I had no place else to go. I walked to the kitchen, looking for something to eat. Ms. Hanks was sitting at the table drinking coffee.

"Hey Shanna, at first you will walk to school, but later a bus will pick you up, ok?" Ms. Hanks explained. "Oh, and Shanna, I'm sorry I forgot to give you your medication, it was in the envelope the worker gave me, and it slipped my mind. You should have reminded me."

I wasn't thinking about my medication.

"You hongry today, huh?" Ms. Hanks said with a smirk.

"Jus' a little," I said.

"Made you some waffles and sausage, they in tha frezza." Ms. Hanks said.

CHAPTER 8

Who Is This?

"You can make me some breakfast too," a male voice said.

I looked around and saw Ron with his shirt off. He was cute. I looked at him and said nothing.

"Naw, I'm jus' playin', wuts yo' name?"

"Shashanna."

"I'm Ron."

"Who is neva home. Boy, put yo' shirt on and leave this girl alone," Ms. Hanks interrupted.

"Dang Ma," Ron went back down the stairs.

"That's my son, Ron, I'm sorry, I neva mention him befo' cuz he's always in tha streets!" Ms. Hanks stressed while washing out her coffee cup and leaving me in the kitchen alone.

I didn't feel like making waffles, so looked in the fridge for something fast and easy.

Ron came back upstairs with a shirt on.

"Where you from, Shanna? Can I call you Shanna, cuz you name is too long."

"I don't care, and I'm from the Westside."

"So you from the bad side of Chicago, huh?" Ron asked.

"Why is everybody saying that?" I said with attitude.

"Gurl, loosen up, I'm jus' playin'."

Suddenly, Ms. Hanks called Ron in the next room. If she was trying to be discreet she failed because I heard everything she said.

"Don't mess with that girl, you know I can get in trouble, I know huh fast ass probably like you."

I poured myself a bowl of cereal. Ron walked by and gave me a smile and went back downstairs. I ate the cereal thinking about Ron instead of my situation. I was stuck, but it was better to be stuck with a cute boy in the basement.

When the girls came back from school they had another girl with them. She was loud and ghetto as hell, just like the girls from my hood. I liked her instantly.

"Oh, this is the new girl, Shashanna. Shashanna, this is Monday." Lenzy blurted out.

I wondered who would name their child after a day of the week.

"Hey Sha! Shashanna!" Monday shouted. "Yea, Imma call you Shanna!"

"That's okay, everybody call me that!" I said.

Monday left the room with Lenzy when Ms. Hanks called them both.

"Ingrid, is Monday y'all friend?" I asked.

"Naw, she's Ms. Hanks' granddaughter and Lenzy's niece." She answered.

Monday came back in the room and said goodbye.

"You seem cool Shanna, don't let Lenzy stress you out. Keep her in check like you been doin'." She winked her eye and left.

I didn't know where this Monday girl was coming from, but she felt like a possible friend.

When Ms. Hanks finally took me to school, I was put in the eighth grade, and I was thrilled; something was going right.

The next day I knew that I had to walk to school, but I didn't know how far. It took us forty-five minutes. We had to walk down blocks that led to a forest. When we got out of the woods we had more blocks to walk before we got to the school. I knew making this walk everyday was going to be a problem. Ingrid and Nancy assured me that once my name got on the list, I would be able to catch the bus with them.

Something else cool did happen though, when we got to the school a bunch of kids knew my name.

"Is yo' name Shanna?" One boy asked.

"Yeah, how you know that?" I asked with suspicion.

The group looked at each other and giggled. The crowd opened up and there was Monday in the middle of them.

"Welcome to my school, Shanna."

I had been introduced as Monday's pretty cousin from a school in the city. The word spread fast, and I was instantly popular, but I also had instant enemies. In one day, I had friends and rivals.

I wasn't expecting what Monday did for me; she broke the ice with the kids, and that made me less introverted. When lunchtime rolled around I had a seat in the cafeteria with Monday.

"Shanna, you see that boy ova there? His name is Earl Bogan, and he is the most popular boy in the school … all the girls like him. I told him about you and how pretty you are. He just broke up with his girlfriend, Sheila; I'll show huh to you later." Monday blabbed.

When I got up to empty my tray everybody had their eyes on me, as if I was someone famous. I walked past Earl's table to see if he would look at me. Not only did he look at me, he grabbed my hand, but I pulled away.

Then his friends started singing the Kool and the Gang song, "Joanna," but they replaced Joanna with Shanna.

"*Sha-shan-na, I love you, Sha-shan-na, I love youuuu, Sha-shan-na I love you.*"

I almost ran back to Monday's table.

"Gurlllll, see what I'm talking 'bout, you betta talk to him. He made them sing you a song," Monday said.

I blushed and felt special, and Earl was cute, but I had cuter boy in the basement. Monday and her crew started laughing and praising me.

"I don't want to talk to him." I said, still smiling from the song.

"Why gurl, he like you," Monday said.

"Yeah, the song was nice, but . . ."

But, my mind was on Ron, the cute boy in the basement.

"You got a boyfriend, don't you?" Melody asked.

"No, no, no."

"Yes you do, I can tell."

All I did was smile.

It wasn't like Ms. Hanks said. Ron was home every day since that morning in the kitchen, and we talked all the time. I looked forward to going to the house because I knew Ron would be there, and that afternoon was no different.

"Hi Ron, what school you go to?" I said while putting my book bag on the kitchen chair.

"I'm in high school. You don't know nothing 'bout that," Ron joked.

"I will next year," I said proudly.

"You still a young buck, and when you get in high school; I would've graduated and gone."

"You a senior in High School?" I asked.

"Yes indeed," Ron said proudly.

"So," I snipped.

"Oh, you got a smart ass mouth, huh?" Ron said while brushing against me.

"Nope. Why you be downstairs a lot?" I asked.

"That's where I sleep. Come here, let me show you something." Ron said while gesturing towards the stairs.

I was excited to finally see Ron's sanctuary, and when I got down there, I was in awe. He had turntables, speakers, posters, and albums everywhere.

"You like them?" Ron asked.

"Yes, are you a DJ or something?"

"I give party's every weekend. That's why my Ma say I'm neva home."

"Can I touch it?" I asked about the closest turntable.

"Yea, but be careful, this shit is expensive."

"Okay," I said carefully.

Ron turned on his equipment and played my favorite song, "Let the Music Play", by Shanon. I couldn't believe he had that song, and I never seen so many records in my entire life. Ron had two of every record. I touched this box that was between the two turntables and asked what it was, and Ron told me it was an equalizer. It switched from one record to another. I sat back and watched Ron work, and he was good, just like the mixes I heard on WBMX. At that moment, I began to feel better about staying in the boondocks, but I still missed Carl.

As I loosened up my personality, I began to flourish, and as I flourished, my popularity began to grow, and I was starting to rebel against Ms. Hanks' rules. Everyone knew my name like that bar called "Cheers", and I began to lose focus on what was important, my grades. Getting up early and those extra-long walks had taken its toll on me, not to mention the medication. Every day, I fell asleep in my eight o'clock class and thought nothing of it. I had my own clique, mostly Monday's friends, but they seemed to cling on to me tighter.

But, there was one thing that would stop me with popularity, sex. Monday and her hot ass friends talked about sex a lot. Not only did they talk the talk, they walked the walk. I got tired of hearing about details of their little sexcapades.

"Shanna, you know what we talking 'bout, right?" Monday asked.

"Yea!" I said nonchalantly.

I felt nervous because I didn't want to reveal that I was a virgin, and I felt like I was the only one who hadn't had sex.

Weeks went by, and I got adjusted to my surroundings, but I didn't improve my grades or stay awake in class; the Epilepsy medicine kept me sleepy in the mornings. I wanted to do something else at school besides just going to class. I figured getting involved in something would make me like going more. I saw a notice for volleyball team tryouts and decided to go. I made the starting lineup and got so excited. I felt good about what I had achieved.

I started participating in my classes, and I tried harder to stay awake in my earlier classes. I had motivation; to stay on the team I had to have at least C's in my classes. Monday and her clique were excited for me for making the team, and we celebrated in the cafeteria.

"Shashanna, kick those white girls' ass when you get out there!" Monday cheered.

"You know I am, Monday!" I said with my hands on my hips.

I looked forward to practice, but after two weeks of being on the team, I got called out of a class.

"Shashanna, can I speak to you in private?" The volleyball coached asked.

I wondered what the coach wanted that was so important she had to get me out of my class. At first, I feared I had to move somewhere else. I was getting familiar with everyone and hoped DCFS wasn't going to make me move.

"Shashanna, I have some bad news. You can't play volleyball because you have Epilepsy, which means you are a risk, I'm sorry." The coach said with regret.

"Is it that I take medication because I can stop taking it?"

"Please, don't do that," The coach said while putting her hand on my shoulder.

"How did y'all find out about that?" I asked.

"It's in your school records, and we should've checked them first before your practice game. I'm very sorry."

And I felt she was, but her sorry ass didn't keep me on the team. I returned to class with my head hanging low. I didn't want to talk to anyone, and I kept my disappointment to myself.

I wanted to feel better, to go the show, or to the store, or something, so I asked Ms. Hanks about my allowance. She hadn't given me a dime since I arrived.

"Ms. Hanks, do I get allowance?"

"Yes, here you go." She handed me two bills.

I looked, and looked again, and it was still a ten and a five.

"Is this all I get, Ms. Hanks?"

"Yep, you only get fifteen dollars a month, and with that you buy your own toilet paper, toothpaste, and deodorant." She said with her bucked eyes popped open.

"What?" She had to be kidding.

Ms. Hanks looked at me and said, "Did I studda?"

At least when I stayed with Beth, she gave Carl and me over a hundred dollars. To come down from over a hundred dollars to fifteen dollars a month wasn't right.

The look on her face told me arguing with her was pointless. I would call the worker in the morning. I put the bills in my pocket and went to my room. The candy store sounded like a good idea to me. In the room was a good surprise. Monday was there.

"Hey," we said at the same time.

"I am spending the weekend with y'all."

All I could do was hug her. I wanted to tell her what happened at school with the volleyball team and with Ms. Hanks, but I didn't because Lenzy was in the room.

Monday and I had grown really close. Ingrid and Nancy were happy about Monday coming over to spend the night too. I found out that night that Ms. Hanks did not like Monday because Monday's mom, Ms. Hanks' daughter, was an alcoholic, and she took out her anger for her daughter on Monday.

Later that night, Lenzy became jealous of Monday and me sitting on the bed talking. She wasn't the center of attention, and that pissed her off. While Monday and I were talking, Lenzy interrupted our conversation and started talking about New Edition while pointing at their poster.

"My boyfriend is Ralph because he is the cutest one. Ingrid, you can have Ronnie, Nancy, you can have Bobby, and Monday you can have Ricky."

"What about Shanna?" Monday asked.

"Fuck huh, she not supposed to be here anyway!" Lenzy said grudgingly.

"Lenzy, not tonight. Keep talking shit, and I'ma shut you up."

"You ain't gonna do shit because you always telling me what you gonna do to me, ain't nothing happen yet!" Lenzy barked.

Lenzy walked over to the bed and stood over me. I didn't wait; I stood up and popped her in the face with my fist as hard as I could. She started swinging fingernails first, and she did manage to scratch my face, but her wild swinging left her face open, and I socked her again, hard. That time the punch knocked her to floor, and she started yelling.

"Momma, Momma, Momma!"

Ms. Hanks ran into the room, "What tha hell is going on here, and why is my baby's lip bleeding?"

It was her lip and her nose.

"Grandma, Lenzy started da fight wit' Shashanna first!" Monday said.

"Shut up, who told you to say sumthin'!" Ms. Hanks silenced Monday.

"She did start the fight wit' me, and I'm tired of huh messin' wit' me . You neva say nothing to huh." I protested to Ms. Hanks.

"Momma, I didn't start nothing. She hit me first and then I hit huh back!" Cried Lenzy.

"Did you hit huh first, Shanna?"

"Yeah because….."

"Because nothing, who gave you tha right to hit my baby? I'm callin yo' worker, and I'm takin' yo' allowance," Ms. Hanks threatened.

"Yea, fifteen dollars, I'm real hurt. Call the worker," I said while rolling my eyes.

"Monday, you have to sleep in anotha room, and when morning come, you gotta get outta here!"

"Grandma., I didn't do nothing!"

"Every time you come round shit happens!" Ms. Hanks shouted.

"But Grandma . . ." Monday said, reaching for Ms. Hanks.

"Don't . . ." Ms. Hanks slapped Monday's hand away from her.

Monday left before I woke up the next morning, and Lenzy was walking around like her shit didn't stink.

I don't recall Christmas Day at Ms. Hanks', but I do remember Valentine's Day. I remember getting all kinds of cards and candies from secret admirers at school. I even gave one of my chocolates to Ms. Hanks, just to get off of her "shit list," but it didn't work.

I continued to watch Ms. Hanks buy Lenzy brand new clothes while she bought us "foster girls" clothes from the thrift store. I personally had taken the fifteen dollars and bought a brand new shirt one month and a pair of pants the next month. I realized that I hadn't had a whipping in months, and that felt good, but there are different types of abuse and neglect.

Valentine's Day night, this really hardcore looking girl came over to the house. She had ashy skin and a bandanna tied around her head.

"This is my susta, she used to live here befo' y'all!" Lenzy boasted, walking the girl into the kitchen.

This girl looked like she been through the system and failed. She looked like she'd just got out of jail.

"Hey Cheryl, how you been?" Ms. Hanks asked.

"Hey Ms. Hanks, I been doing good. I miss y'all!" The hardcore girl said.

"Make yo'self at home!" Ms. Hanks said.

While we sat at the kitchen with the girl, I started feeling uneasy because she kept eyeballing me, and I was getting scared. I smelled a rat with this girl. Ingrid, Nancy, and me left her at the table with Lenzy and Ms. Hanks.

In the bedroom Ingrid said, "I don't like her. I hope she's not spending the night."

"She is, you heard Ms. Hanks tell her to make herself at home," Nancy answered.

It was laundry night and my turn to go first, so I was gathering my clothes for the wash.

Walking through the kitchen to stairs to the basement, the hardcore girl, who was sitting at the table with Lenzy and Ms. Hanks said, "Hey, I heard you hit my susta."

Neither Ms. Hanks nor Lenza looked up. Since they didn't say anything, I didn't either.

I walked away because Cheryl looked scary, and I knew she was older than me. In the basement, I put my clothes in the washer and was heading back upstairs. When I turned around, the girl was in my face.

"I don't like yo' ass, and I'm finna fuck you up! Now what you gonna do?"

Fear had a hold of my mouth. I tried to step around her, but all of a sudden she pushed me against the washer and pulled out a knife and pressed it across my neck, hard.

"You ain't sayin' shit now, is you!"

Instead, looking at the knife, I watched Cheryl tucking her lips into her mouth.

"I should kill yo' ass right now!"

I was in the eighth grade, I was too young to die so, I swallowed hard, and I prayed. All of a sudden Ron was there.

"What the fuck you doing, Cheryl?"

He slung her from me, pinned her down, and started slapping her. He yanked her up from the floor and dragged her to basement door.

"Get yo' ass out of this house, and don't bring yo' ass back!"

"But Momma said I could stay here for a while!"

"Get yo' ass out of here, and my Momma ain't yo' Momma!" He threw her out, and slammed the door behind her. "You alright Shanna?" He walked over to me.

"Yeah," I said while shaking.

"What happened?" Ron asked.

"She tried to kill me because I hit Lenzy."

"Ok, I'm gonna tell Momma what had happen." Ron said.

"Can I stay down here with you for a minute?"

"Yeah, come chill with me." We sat on his bed with his arm around me. I stopped shaking.

"I got a big party tomorrow night. Two suburbs getting together to throw one party, and they hired me. It should be over a thousand people there."

I was impressed, even though I had never been to a real party

"Will you take me?"

"Huh?"

"I mean, can I go?"

"You have to ask Momma because you are only thirteen, and you have a curfew."

"Why don't you ask, huh? I know what she gone say if I ask, pleeeeeeze!" I asked with my hands together as if praying.

"I don't know."

"Monday told me she go to yo' parties, and we the same age."

"That's because my susta let huh do whateva she want to do. Ok, I will ask, but if she say no I ain't asking again."

I screamed, "Yeh!" and kissed him on cheek.

Ms. Hanks said yes, and I was too happy to get out of the house and hang out with Ron. I started going to Ron's parties every weekend, but I started missing my curfew and coming in later and later.

At these parties, I met kids who smoked weed, and with me being young and new to the group, it didn't take much to get me smoking. Sometimes I wouldn't get home until four in the morning.

I remember when "White Horse" by Laid Back came out, and everyone snapped because it had explicit lyrics, *"If you wanna be rich, you gotta be bitch!"* I continued to fail my classes and didn't care because I knew I was going to a party the following weekend, and that was all I cared about. I started smoking weed not only on the weekends, but whenever I could.

Monday brought weed to school, and we smoked it before and after class. We thought we were having the time of our lives. Ms. Hanks noticed the change in my behavior, but she never addressed me personally, she went through Ron.

It was after one of his parties when she initially approached him. We were both surprised that she was up that late. Ms. Hanks told him she wanted to talk in her room. All of a sudden, I heard arguing, and my name was mentioned several times. Ron stormed out of his mother's room and slammed the door. He looked at me in passing and told me I couldn't go to his parties anymore. I thought to myself, *yes the hell I can*, because I'd just started having fun, and I wasn't going to let it end. I got creative.

The next morning while Ms. Hanks was making her coffee, I went into the kitchen and informed her that, "My neck still hurts from the knife Cheryl tried to kill me with."

I knew she didn't want anyone to find out about the incident. Ms. Hanks looked at me and turned the fire on under the kettle.

"Maybe I should call the worker for a doctor's appointment?" I said.

She opened the jar of instant coffee and spooned two teaspoons into her mug.

"What is it you want, Shanna?"

"Can I spend the night over Monday house, she want me to braid huh hair."

"When?" Ms. Hanks asked in a mean tone.
"This Friday."
"Okay, but I'ma drop you off and pick you up the next day."
"Thanks!"

For about a month, I'd made up different reasons why Monday wanted me over. I knew Ron saw me at his parties. He never said anything to Ms. Hanks, but he stopped talking to me altogether. I hated the silence that was between us, so I started making friends with people Ron knew, which was everybody, especially the girls.

Girls wanted Ron so badly that they would give me gifts like Michael Jackson buttons and joints to try to get next to him. We weren't on speaking terms, but the girls didn't know that. I had finally had enough of his silence.

I walked over to Ron while he was spinning records at a party and asked him why he was giving me the silent treatment, and he told me he didn't appreciate my defiance against his mother, and he didn't want anything to do with the situation.

I took that to mean he didn't want anything to do with me, so I said, "Ron, these girls been tryin' to get wit' you."

"What girls?" He asked while looking around.

I brought a few of them over to his D.J. table. He smiled and told me to get their numbers, so I did. I thought by getting girls' numbers that would get him to talk to me. I was that desperate.

The next day, one of the girl's came over to the house. She thanked me for giving Ron her number. I frowned as he took her down to his room. I paced the floor thinking of a reason to go down stairs to interrupt them, so I gathered all my dirty clothes and brought them to the laundry room. I had to pass Ron's room to get to the washer and dryer. Apparently, they had already started something because the girl hurried and pulled the covers up when she saw me. Ron came in the laundry room and asked me what I was doing.

"I'm washing my clothes, what you think?"

"Right now, Shanna!" Ron said while half dressed.

"I was gonna wash my clothes befo' y'all got here," I said while fidgeting with my clothes.

Ron looked at me suspiciously as I looked the opposite way.

"Okay, since you down here, you can watch. Imma close tha doors, and you can look through the shutters." Ron said.

While I watched Ron having sex with that girl, he would turn and look at me while fucking her. I didn't know what to think. I was watching the boy I liked fuck another girl. I was traumatized.

While my crush for Ron had gotten stronger, my grades were getting weaker, but I still got my party on. I continued to party every weekend and got wasted every chance I got.

I wanted to get back at Ron for fucking that girl in front of me, so I went to a party with his best friend, Neal. Ron was the DJ. When he played a slow grind record, I positioned us right in front of him. I proceeded to slow grind with Neil under the blue lights in the basement. I looked over at Ron, and he acted like it didn't bother him, so I kissed Neil, and that's when Ron came over and grabbed me and cursed me out.

"You jealous or sumthin'?" I snapped.

"You need to carry yo' drunk ass home because you know you in trouble wit' my momma, right? You need to get yo' shit together befo' you have to move!" Ron screamed. "Don't you understand, she ain't got to keep you?"

I pulled away from Ron, but I was drunk, so I tripped over a white plastic pipe, but struggled to get up, which caused me to fall on two other pipes and suddenly shit and water spewed out over everything and everybody. Kids were frantically running over each other, trying to get out of that basement.

I went home with Monday and spent the night over at her house. Since Monday's Mom was an alcoholic, we'd walk in without explaining where we've been, she was cool.

When we woke up the next morning, it was April 1st, the day Marvin Gaye was killed by his father. When Monday and I heard the news on the radio, we thought it was an April fool's joke and didn't believe it.

"Awwh, hell naw, for real!"

"Monday, you know they lyin' because it's April Fool's day!" I said.

"Oh, yeah!"

Later, we discovered the truth, and it was reason enough to get wasted and mourn the death of one of the greatest artists ever. From Monday's house, I went over to Neil's because I didn't want to go back to Ms. Hanks' house yet. Ron was mad at me, so I went over his best friend's house.

When I got there, we went straight to his bedroom and started kissing, and I thought since everybody was juicing, what we called sex back in the day, then I should too.

"Come on, let's do it," I demanded.

We continued to kiss, and Neil reached between my legs and started to rub my girly part.

Then he whispered, "You have to take your clothes off to do it."

I instantly became nervous and started to shake.

"Don't be nervous," he whispered.

"I'm ok."

Neil took the liberty to take off his clothes first while I watched and then he pulled down his underwear, and when I saw his thang I cringed and became nervous all over again.

"You don't have to do anything you don't want to do, OK." Neil said.

Since he was stroking his Johnson so intensely, I knew he wanted some badly, so I slowly took my clothes off and quickly got under the covers. We started kissing again, but this time we were both naked, and his thang was poking the hell out of me.

"You sure you wanna do this?" Neil asked.

I nodded my head and said, "Yes."

Neil reached over to his nightstand drawer and got a condom then he ripped it open with his teeth. While Neil rolled the condom on his thang, my heart started beating faster and harder.

"Are you alright?" Neil asked.

"Mmmmm hmmmmm."

Neil parted my legs and rubbed his thang up and down and then… Nothing. He was so big, and I was so tight that Neil was unable to put it in, so he gave up.

But what was funny at the time, was that I thought we did it because it was painful. I called Monday and told her that I finally did it, and I was in their sex club.

When I finally made it Ms. Hanks house, my bags were sitting by the front door, packed and ready to go.

"I'm 'bout to call yo' worker so she can come and get yo' ass!" Ms. Hanks ranted.

I did not say a word because Ron told me that this was going to happen, so I wasn't surprised. Ron looked at me as if to say that he was disappointed, but I didn't care anymore about what he thought, so I gave him a disappointed look in return. I waited on the couch for what seemed like forever because I wanted to leave right away. Finally, the worker came to the house to carry me to my new place of residence; wherever it was.

Ms. Hanks told the worker how patient she had been with me, but she had reached her limit. I thought about how patient I was with her ass too, for giving fifteen dollars a month and having to buy toiletries with the money, and she'd set me up to get beat by her old foster girl. I brushed everything off, and left the drama in Ms. Hanks' living room, and I moved on.

CHAPTER 9

Pit Stop

I vaguely remember details about the place the worker drove me to. There was a senior couple who had a German Shepherd dog that stayed in the kitchen. I guess to guard the refrigerator because I had to get permission to go in it. The man of the house smoked cigars, and I hated cigars and dogs. The lady of the house was quiet and stayed in her room most of the time. I was the only kid in the house, the good part was I continued to go to the same school and get high with Monday and her friends, but I couldn't go to any parties. I felt like I had moved from one messed up situation to another. I didn't stay at this place a month.

The next temporary site was in Harvey, Illinois. This home had a couple of boys living there, and I was the only female. The foster mother told me up front that I'd be staying temporarily, which was cool with me because I was still hoping to live with Carl again; being around boys made me miss him more.

I asked the worker about living with him again, but she said she didn't know. I told her I missed my brother, and she gave me a diary. I didn't understand what missing my brother had to with a diary, but I started writing in it. It was like talking to a friend. I wrote down my thoughts every night.

I didn't go to school in Harvey, so no old friends and no smoking weed. It was just me and my diary until the worker came to get me again. When I gathered my stuff to leave, I discovered my diary was missing. I was pissed, but there was nothing I could do about it.

CHAPTER 10

Holy Hell

The ride to the next home was a long one. We were heading back to Chicago by the expressway signs. All I thought about was seeing my brother. On the ride there, the worker told me this wasn't a temporary site. I didn't know what to expect, but I didn't expect what I saw. When the foster mother opened the door, her oversized wig jumped out at me. She looked like Rick James. I wanted to laugh, but I kept my composure and walked in the home full of curiosity.

I sat and watched as the worker and the foster parent filled out paper work. The worker left without introducing me. The foster mother introduced herself and laid out the rules. Her name was Ms. Rolland, and she told me that her home was saved and sanctified, and I had to attend bible study every week in order to stay in her home.

"The kitchen is off limits afta five o'clock. You must be in the house befo' it get dark. Everyone have chores around here, and I'll let you know what you have to do soon. Your name is Shanna, right?" Ms. Rolland asked while her wig was moving with every word.

"It's Shashanna, but you can call me Shanna."

"Shanna, did you understand the rules?"

"Yea."

Ms. Rolland helped me to bring my clothes upstairs to settle in. The upstairs was an attic turned into a living space. There were three bedrooms and a bathroom, and Ms. Rolland directed me to the room that I would sleep in.

"This is yo' dressa draw, and you have another girl who sleep in here wit' you."

Ms. Rolland left me upstairs to unpack, and I took the liberty of looking around. I wondered how many other girls stayed there.

The first girl came home. She was in high school, and her name was Altavese; we were roommates.

"Hi, what's yo' name!" Alatavese asked.

"Shashanna."

"Hi Shashanna, Tammie, and Noel will be home soon. They are Ms. Rolland's daughters," she explained, "I have to make a quick run, but I will be back."

She left me alone in the attic. When the other two girls and Ms. Rolland came upstairs, we all smiled at each other. We were feeling each other out with glances until Ms. Rolland broke the ice.

"These are my daughters, Noel and Tammie. This is Shashanna. Can they call you Shanna?" Asked Ms. Rolland.

"Yeah," I said, trying to look as friendly as possible

"Did you meet Altavese?"

"Yes, I did."

Ms. Rolland's girls looked me over and said their hello's and went back downstairs with her. I was alone in the sitting area until Altavese came back with her arms full of books.

Right away I asked her, "Do you know how to get to the Westside?"

"Yeah, why?"

"That's where I am from, and my brother still lives there. I want to see him."

"No problem, we can make that happened," and she gave me a big warm smile.

We became cool right away.

I could tell this house was strict because it was quiet. When the sisters came back upstairs, they sat in the sitting area with me but hardly talked; no questions or anything. Since they didn't ask any, I didn't either until I got hungry.

"What time do we eat?"

"My momma will call us when dinner is ready," Ms. Rolland's oldest daughter Noel said.

She spoke softly with braces on her teeth, and she had bad acne.

"What color is you?" The younger sister, Tammie, asked.

"Black!" I snipped.

"You ain't black, look at yo' skin," she was serious.

I told her what Beth told me, "My daddy was Puerto Rican, so I am light skinned. But, I am Black because my mama is Black, ok?"

"Ok," she said and looked back at the television.

A foul smell rolled through the sitting area.

"Y'all smell that?" I asked. It smelled like piss. "Who peed in the bed because I smell pee?" I said while holding my nose.

Altavese looked at me as if to say, be quiet. No one said anything. I began to notice that the smell was coming out of the sister's room. I guessed Tammie since she was the youngest, but she was twelve. The whole upstairs was permeated with the stench of urine.

I was waiting on dinner, hoping that Tammie would close her bedroom door and keep the piss smell in her room, but she didn't, and I had to hold my nose and suffer.

After dinner, Ms. Rolland felt the need to repeat her house rules to me, and she assigned me my chore.

"There will be bible study every Wednesday, no eating after five, and everyone has chores around here. Shanna, you can start with the dishes tomorrow," Ms. Rolland repeated.

I hated washing dishes, but I said, "Ok," and went upstairs.

"Damn!" I said when we got upstairs.

I held my nose until I made it in my bedroom and closed the door.

"Tammie don't like you," Altavese exclaimed.

"I don't care. Do she eva change huh bed?" I asked.

"Girl, you will get used to it!" Altavese said while waving her hand. "Where did you stay befo' you came here?"

"Chicago Heights, but only a little while."

"But, you from the Westside?" Altavese inquired.

"Yeah, and my brother is still there."

"I used to stay on the Westside. I know my way there."

Altavese told me what high school she attended and what school I would go to.

"I know you are wondering about Ms. Rolland. She's cool, but she is very religious, and you gone have to go to her bible classes that she have downstairs."

"Downstairs," I said in disbelief.

"Yep, huh and her church friends meet downstairs, and they speak in tongues."

"Speak in tongues?"

Altavese laughed and said, "You will see."

"When something go wrong around here, she speak in tongue, it's so funny! What songs do you like?"

"I like a lot of songs!" I said quickly. I wanted Altavese to shut up. Smelling piss, tasteless food, and her talking were adding up to a headache for me. "I have a head ache, and I need to sleep. Ok, Altavese?"

"Okay, goodnight," she said politely.

"Goodnight."

The next morning Ms. Rolland came upstairs to wake me up for breakfast; everyone had left for school. I must have been tired because I can hear a pen drop when I sleep, but I heard nothing.

"After you get finish eating, wash the dishes, ok?" Ms. Rolland said sternly.

"Okay," I answered.

I ate and washed the dishes, and I went upstairs to take a shower and finish unpacking my things. From the things Altavese told me about Ms. Rolland, I was turned off with living at the house, but the thought of living closer to my Brother made me happy. I needed Altavese to get me to the Westside, but Carl was closer than he had been in a long time.

Ms. Rolland called me from downstairs.

"Shanna, you will start going to the same school, Noel, and Tammie is goin' to, ok?" Ms. Rolland felt the need to explain everything . . . a few times.

"Okay."

I wondered what the new school would be like. I had to start all over again with making friends. When I went back upstairs to watch television, I made sure to close the sister's bedroom door; it helped some, but the piss smell was ever present. Later, the girls came home, but they had to go downstairs and clean up for the bible study meeting.

When I went down stairs for bible study, Noel said, "Shashanna, my momma told me to give you this Bible to read," while holding her head down.

I took the Good Book, but I knew I wasn't going to read it because someone ordered me to do so. All of the sanctified people gathered in Ms. Rolland's front room and held hands in prayer. I looked and knew right then that I wasn't going to participate in this event because I didn't feel good about it.

Everybody started speaking in tongues just like Altavese warned me, and it scared me. The chants sounded like zombie noises or something spooky. I had never heard language like that.

"O - idioshundahaha,"

At first, I thought they were pronouncing my name wrong, but no one was looking in my direction. When the bible study was over, I all but ran upstairs. School would be a welcomed diversion.

The first thing I noticed at the school was the diversity; there were whites, Puerto Ricans, Mexicans, and Blacks. I knew that I would like the school because there were others who had the same skin color as me. I was thinking I wouldn't stand out as much, and I was right.

"You not Mexicano, what is you? You have the hair and body, I don't understand." One of the Hispanic students asked in disbelief.

"I'm half Puerto Rican and half Black."

"Oh, okay," the student said.

That answer satisfied the Puerto Ricans and Mexicans but not the Blacks. They still wanted to call me white. There were Black kids at this school, but they were the minority, which made them more approachable. Most of the Black guys thought I was Spanish at first because the Puerto Ricans and Mexicans started speaking Spanish to me, but when I couldn't answer, they saw I was Black and that made them happy. I made friends fast.

The school must have been built in the 1800's because the chairs where attached to the desk and the chalkboards where black instead of green, but as long as I was in the eighth grade I didn't care. The whole school smelled like old library books. The teachers were just as old as the school, which meant they didn't have the energy to discipline. So school was cool, but my home was a different story.

On Wednesday, the house became invaded with sanctified church folks. When Bible service began there was a silence, we held hands and prayed. After the prayer, the talking in tongues began, and it always scared me. I wanted to stop going to bible study, but attending service was one of Ms. Rolland's house rules.

One Wednesday Ms. Rolland asked, "Shanna, did you like service today?"

"Ummmm, yeah," I said.

"What did you like about it?"

"I like holding people's hands and reading, but why did everybody have on dresses, and they weren't in church?" I asked.

"Shanna, sanctified women wear dresses all the time, no exceptions."

Ms. Rolland felt compelled to sit me down and talk about the whole sanctified religious experience, and everything went in one ear and out the other. After seeing and hearing her speak in tongue with the others, I categorized her as crazy in my mind.

Upstairs in our bedroom Altavese said, "I told you that shit is weird, gurl!"

"Altavese, I don't know how much more I can take. Do the classes ever get cancelled?"

"Neva, she has them like clockwork."

"Well, I don't think it's right for huh to make us do something we don't want to do."

"I know, right!" Altavese concurred.

In bed that night, I thought that Ms. Rolland's was only a little better than Ms. Holmes.' Eventually, I did adjust to most of Ms. Rolland's strict rules, and I got used to the pissy stench and Bible study Wednesdays.

I liked my new school because I made lots of friends, Black and Spanish. I can recall this guy named Stan who wasn't Spanish, but his skin was red, and his eyes were hazel and his hair was red.

His approach was equivalent to a bully, "Hey gurl, wuts yo' name?"

"Shashanna, why?" I snipped.

"You new here ain't you?"

"Duh, yeah," I said.

"You a smart ass ain't you?" He asked with his hands on his hips. "Well, I like you, and you gone hang out wit' me, got it?" He insisted.

I had never been bullied into hanging out with a person. I laughed at him, and agreed.

"My name is Stan, and I already know who you is."

By Stan's body language and hand gestures, I knew that he was gay, but he denied it to others who suspected the same, so I never asked him about his sexuality. Stan introduced me to his crew, one in particular that I liked was this girl named Nydia; she struck me as cool from the start. Nydia was versatile with her wardrobe and hair, she was so stylish and wore make up… I was in awe of her.

"Nydia, this is Shanna, Shanna this is Nydia!" Stan introduced the two of us in front of his locker.

"Hello Shanna!" Nydia said with her Spanish accent.

I was amazed.

"Hi."

Then Nydia started to speak Spanish to me. I didn't want to disappoint her, but I shrugged my shoulders to gesture that I didn't understand her. I got tired of Hispanic kids speaking Spanish to me and I couldn't respond, so I asked Nydia, how do I say... "I don't speak Spanish" in Spanish.

"No hablo Espanol," Nydia said slowly.

I had Nydia to repeat it every time I saw her until I got it right; I also, learned curse words in Spanish too. Nydia and I became instant hommies. She invited me to eat lunch at her table and gave me these black rubbery friend ship bracelets. I cherished those bracelets so that they wore off about three years later because I wouldn't take them off for anything. After Nydia had given me the friendship bracelets, I must have gotten a thousand more from other Hispanic girls because Nydia was the popular girl at the school, so others followed her. Me, Stan, and Nydia hung out at school a lot, and when you saw one you saw all three of us. School was a breeze.

I remember not doing my class assignments, but I socialized and pretended that I did my work. I started hanging out a little more than usual, and I found the kids that smoked weed. Being fourteen in the eighth grade, I was leery who I revealed my love for weed to, so I waited until someone approached me. I managed to drag myself in the house and obeyed the strict rules, but the girls were wondering where I was spending my time, especially Altavese.

"Shanna, where you be going after school? I don't see you until it's time to come in the house."

"I jus' hang out wit' my friends at school, don't you have friends at yo' school?" I asked.

"Yea, but I don't like them that much."

"You can hang out wit' me and my friends," I offered.

"Y'all too young." Altavese said frowning. "I just asked."

The more fun I had, the less I felt obligated to do my weekly chores that Ms. Rolland posted on the refrigerator door. I hated coming home from a good time to clean up. Ms. Rolland noticed that I stopped coming straight home from school and started breaking the rules of her house.

"Why don't you come straight home just like everybody else?" Ms. Rolland asked with her Rick James lips.

"I don't know." I answered.

"Well, you gonna have to start or you gonna be on punishment. Just because you new here, don't mean that you can do whateva you want. You have to abide by my rules just like everybody else. You got that, Shanna?" Ms. Rolland's face and her big wig were moving in opposite directions.

"Yeah," I said with no sincerity.

I hated to be confined, so I told her that I would comply by her rules. I knew if I didn't do what Ms. Rolland asked me to do I would have to move and loose the chance to see Carl, because I could end up in the suburbs again. I stayed cool about a month or so and did what I was told. I made it home after school and did my assigned chores.

I became impatient with Ms. Rolland and her rules and bedwetting daughter, Tammie. The rules and the scent of piss were choking me. I was a free spirited kid who wanted to get high. Stan, Nydia and I got tight as hell. They waited for me to come outside after chores so we could hang out and smoke weed. Stan didn't indulge in weed smoking like Nydia and me, but we were still close.

One day, this Hispanic guy who was friends with Nydia invited me to a break dancing competition. We went and watched him do his thing. His crew won the contest. He then asked me to meet him alone later.

"Gurl, I think he likes you, you betta meet him," Nydia encouraged.

"What's his name?"

"His name is Angel, the cutest boy in the neighborhood. He's so calente!" Nydia kissed her fingers.

"Okay Nydia, what is that?" I asked.

"He's hot!"

I had cooled off on boys and wasn't into them as much as Nydia, but I agreed to meet with Angel later. When we met, he led me to a garage in the back of an alley. I thought he was going to perform a private break dance for me. We went into the garage and there was a dirty pissed on mattress. He started kissing me and feeling on me. I stopped him.

"What do you want with me?" I said after I push him away.

"I like you, and I think you pretty," Angel said in his thick Spanish accent.

We kissed again, and before I knew it, Angel motioned towards the dirty mattress.

"What, you want me to lay on that dirty thang?"

"Yeah, why not?"

"Hell naw, nope, no, and hell naw."

Angel got angry and left me in the garage. I had to find my way home because it was dark, and I was late for curfew. When I got home, I got in trouble as soon as I stepped my foot in the door.

"I told you the next time you come in late, you was gonna be on punishment," Ms. Rolland met me at the door.

"I didn't try to come in late, Ms. Rolland, don't put me on punishment," I pleaded.

"I gave you plenty of chances to get it right. You on punishment for two weeks."

I wanted to defend myself, but I didn't want to reveal why I was late, so I took my punishment without a fight.

"Shanna, next time you pull something like this I will call yo' worker, you got it?" That was Ms. Rolland's favorite line.

"Yeah."

Spending time restricted to the attic made me reflect on how much I missed my brother and not getting enough money for allowance. I was getting the same fifteen dollars but didn't have to buy toiletries with it. Being on punishment meant staying upstairs with the pissy smell or going down stairs and listen to Ms. Rolland talk to me about her version of what God wanted me to do. Every day of the punishment the Bible was read to me. Bible study Wednesday approached, and my attitude was nasty. I refused to attend despite her orders. After everyone left Bible study, Ms. Rolland came upstairs and yelled at me.

"Go downstairs and clean up afta everybody then clean the breezeway."

I wanted to curse Ms. Rolland out for yelling at me, but I remembered the plan to see Carl and the importance of staying in the city. Ms. Rolland had a cat and kittens in the breezeway, and while I was sweeping, they were in my way. Being as angry as I was, I picked the kittens up and put them in the freezer and continued to sweep the carpet. When I finished, I forgot about the kittens in the freezer.

Ms. Rolland yelled upstairs, "Shashanna!"

"What? I cleaned up," I yelled back.

"Get down here, right now," Ms. Rolland was standing in front of the freezer, "Look! Why did you do that?"

The three kittens were shivering and barely alive.

"They were in the way while I was sweeping,"

After my response, she just stared at me, "That was cruel, Shanna."

Ms. Rolland shook her head and took the kittens from the freezer and held them to her chest. She went in her room, closed the door, and left me standing where I was.

That was not her typical response. I began to think I was in real trouble and started to alleviate the trouble by crying. Talking to her bedroom door, I told Ms. Rolland how sorry I was.

She yelled through the door for me to go upstairs and that she would talk to me later. Everybody was quiet and looked at me as if they were afraid for me. I sat on my bed and waited for Ms. Rolland to call me back downstairs.

"Shanna!"

Altavese, Noel, and Tammie looked at me as if the jury had reached its verdict, and I was found guilty; immediately I went downstairs to apologize.

"Ms. Rolland, I'm sorry, and I won't do it again! Do I have to leave?" I cried.

"Tomorrow we gone have to see yo' worker because what you did was nothing but tha devil, and I don't want devils in my house."

"Please. I promise not to disobey you again. That wuz the devil, not me."

I knew I had to lean on religion for to give me another chance. She looked at me and immediately pulled out her Bible.

"Get on your knees and I will ask the Lord to forgive you for your sins, now."

Ms. Rolland sounded like she was praying, but her eyes were wide open. She began sprinkling me with oil and then she just poured it over my forehead.

"It's unclean, the spirit is unclean. Break the yolk of evil flowing through this chile veins ….o'idioshundahuhhuh!"

I was scared as hell, but I joined in prayer, "Lord, please forgive me, take this devil out of me . . . please."

I dropped facedown to the carpet, going along with everything and hoping Ms. Rolland would forgive me and give me another chance.

"Yes, yes Lord, yes Lord, yes. Shanna, if the Lord can forgive you, so can I."

I said, "Thank ya Jesus," and meant it.

CHAPTER 11

Guess Who?

I didn't have to leave Ms. Rolland's home or cancel my plans to see my brother, but I still had to go downtown to see my worker for a six-month evaluation, which I hated.

When we got down there, I was overwhelmed with questions such as: "Are you doing any drugs? How are you doing in school?"

I always answered questions as candid as I possibly could. I admitted to smoking weed, and I was doing ok in school. The round table of people looked at each other and then talked amongst each other while I sat and waited for their responses. Then they asked Ms. Rolland about my behavior in her home, she paused and said that I needed some additional help; her and my worker had taken the liberty of contacting my mother.

At first, I wasn't paying attention, until Ms. Rolland mentioned my mom. I looked up as if someone poked me with a pencil. My mom and her boyfriend walked in as if they were coming to save me.

My mom was there . . . Ms. Rolland and the worker could reach my mom, and I couldn't. She sat at the table like she was not missing from my life.

What the fuck - was the question in my mind.

They spoke to each other like it was nothing new; my mom, my worker, and Ms. Rolland nodded at each other and shook hands.

My mom knowing them meant that she knew where I was. Then why the fuck was I a foster child? I was confused and angry. My mom tried to hug me, but I drew away. Did she know where Carl was too?

I sat at that table listening to these people talk about how messed up I was and how they were going to help me. I wanted to scream, but I was too angry.

"Shashanna, we decided that spending time with your mother will help develop a relationship between the two of you and that will help your behavior."

Then it clicked, the meeting was about the kittens, not my six-month checkup or me being a foster child. The meeting was for the kittens; the people at the table and my mama thought I was crazy.

One of the people told my mama, "Ms. Wilson, we think that Shashanna needs you right now because the system isn't working."

"Shanna, what's going on with you?" My mother asked.

"The other day Shanna had got mad with me and put my kittens in tha freeza." Ms. Rolland snitched.

"You what?" My mother asked.

I refused to look at my mother let alone dignify her question with an answer.

"Shanna, say something to yo' mother because you are hurting her right now." Ms. Rolland said.

My mother began to cry, and I was thinking, *good*. I wanted everybody to hurt. They were all connected, my mama, the worker, and Ms. Rolland. My mama knew where I was all the time. I was glad she was crying.

"Shanna, would you like to visit with your mother?" One of the people at the table asked.

I looked at my mama and the man that had his arm around her shoulders. Did I want to visit her? That was a stupid question. Yes, I wanted to visit my mama, my grandmother, and my brother.

"They talkin' 'bout every weekend, Shanna," Ms Rolland said.

I realized that there was a plan, and everybody in the room knew it but me.

"I don't care."

"Yo' momma is going to call me to let me know when she can come and pick you up."

I wanted to be with my mother, but my anger would not let me show that. I left the meeting end without hugging her or saying a word to her. But inside, I was looking forward to those weekends.

After the meeting, my thinking changed. Life seemed bigger to me, and I seemed smaller. I felt like it was a lot going on that I didn't know about.

One of those people said, "The system failed me."

I was part of a system, and I didn't really understand, but I did know that people were looking at how I behaved.

I went to school and started doing my work, and I made it home on time. I even did my chores without being asked. Once I settled down, I caught on to the schoolwork easy enough. It felt good doing the stuff people expected me to do. Then one day, Ms. Rolland called me down to her room.

"The people at the agency okayed your weekend visits with yo' mom," she said smiling. "You will get to know her, and hopefully you will get to live with her if the visits go well."

"I would get to stay wit' my momma for good?" I asked.

"Yes," Ms. Rolland answered with glee as if she was giving me the gift of my life.

I really didn't know what to think or feel.

"When do I get to go to my momma's house?" I asked.

"This Friday."

That was two days away.

Once, when I lived with Beth, a worker told me she denied my mother's request for visitation because she was unstable due to drug usage. I didn't understand what she said, but that was the last time I had heard anything about my mother. Thoughts of my mother and living with her raced through my head like rapid waters, so I couldn't sleep. When Friday arrived, I went to school as usual, and I anxiously waited for two-thirty to roll around. When I got to the house, I went upstairs and packed my clothes in a plastic bag and waited for my mother.

"Shanna, yo' mother is here!"

I wanted to play it cool, but I didn't. I ran downstairs dragging my bag behind me. When I got to the kitchen my mother stood extending her arms to hug me, but I was still resistant. I wanted to hug her, but I couldn't.

"Shanna," she cried.

"It's okay, let her have her space," my mother's boyfriend said.

"Shanna, this is my boyfriend Lester. Lester, Shanna," Momma introduced us.

"Y'all take care, Shanna be good!" Ms. Rolland scurried us out.

We took the public transportation to my mom's house, which was awkward because no one said anything to each other the whole ride. When we finally made it to our destination, I looked up and thought my mother was joking. We were at a place that looked like a hotel, and it was. There was a guy behind a thick glass with an opening big enough for someone to put a hand though. We walked past the front desk and walked up a flight of stairs to my mom's apartment, which was just a room: a room with four walls, no kitchen, bathroom, just a bed, and a chair. I wasn't impressed at all.

"It's not much, Shanna, but I'm doing the best I can," Momma said.

"Where I'm gonna sleep, and where is the bathroom?" I asked.

"You gonna sleep in the bed while me and Lester sleep on the floor, and the bathroom is down the hall."

Disgusting was the word in my head.

"Shashanna, are you hungry because I can fix you a hamburger on this hot plate."

"No, I'm not hungry."

I sat on the bed and watched the small black and white television and noticed that there was a cat in the room. It made me think about the kittens that got all of this started. The frisky cat approached me only enough to sniff.

"You like her?" My mother asked.

I shook my head yes. My mother tried to get me to have a conversation with her, but I was stubborn and remained quiet.

"You smoke weed?" She asked.

I hadn't in a while. I was trying to be good to get to visit her and do all the right stuff I was supposed to do.

"Sometimes, a little," I said.

"Awwh, I got your attention now."

She finished cooking the hamburgers and placed them in a white plastic bowl. She sat on the bed next to me and opened a Folgers coffee can with weed in it. She rolled up a couple of joints. She lit one, hit it, and passed it to me. I took a hit or two of the joint and started to cough.

"This some good stuff right here, take another hit."

I guessed my mother thought she had to fire up a joint to get a conversation out of me, it worked, but only a little. As the day went on, we talked and laughed a little. Our first weekend went smooth because of weed. The next weekend we smoked less weed and talked more. Each weekend we got closer and closer, like friends, but not the type of closeness that could repair our torn family, but the closeness that allowed us to talk about shit that didn't matter. She never asked me about Carl, and that bugged me.

Back at Ms. Rolland's, I decided it was time to see my brother, so I approached Altavise in the attic.

"I was wondering when you was gonna ask me. I thought you didn't like me anymore or something," Altavise said with her hands on her hips.

"Naw, I don't like being here. I'm sorry to make you feel like that." I explained.

"We can go tomorrow afta school."

"I have to come straight home remember?" I said.

"I got you covered. I'll tell Ms. Rolland that you are going to Bible study wit' me, ok!" Altavese winked her eye.

"Okay!"

"I been going to Bible study at other churches, and Ms. Rolland love it," she said.

I didn't ask had she been going to other churches or just lying to hangout because I really didn't care; as long as she could get me to Carl, she was cool with me.

I was filled with anticipation and excitement, and the thought of me seeing my brother made my heart smile. I couldn't fall asleep right away, but eventually I did. I got up the next morning feeling great; I spoke to everyone, knowing it was going to be a good day. Even the stench of piss coming from Tammie's room didn't get to me. I went to school with pep in my step and looked forward to two-thirty.

My friends stopped me in the hall, "Shanna, what's going on wit' you? You in a good mood."

I told Nydia and Stan that I was going to see my brother, and that I hadn't seen him in a long time.

"You have a brother?" Stan asked in amazement.

"Yep, and I can't wait to see him."

"I thought we were cool, and you didn't tell me you had a brother!"

"Stan, we cool, but it never crossed my mind, I'm sorry."

Two-thirty had come, and I ran out of the building. Altavese met me in the school's playground, and we walked to the bus stop and got on the first bus that went to the el' train.

"Where did you say yo' brother stayed?"

"On Adams and St. Louis."

"That means that we have to get off on Homan and walk a few blocks, that's not bad." Altavese said with confidence.

On the train, I was getting more and more excited seeing buildings I remembered.

Then I heard, "Homan, next stop, Homan Avenue."

When we got off the train, the first thing I saw was Garfield Park, and I wanted to scream because I missed my old neighborhood. As we walked, I told Altavese about each place we passed. When we got to Beth's house, Granma opened the door with her wig off showing her baldhead.

"Heyyyyy Shanna!"

"Hi, Granma!"

Granma hugged and kissed me.

After she asked how I was doing she told me that Beth wasn't home. I introduced Altavese to Granma, and we sat in the roach infested apartment.

"Where is Carl, Granma?"

"He don't stay here nomo, nobody told you?"

"Naw, ain't nobody told me nothing."

"He might be outside wit' his friends, he still come by."

"Okay, come on Altavese."

I went outside, and the first person I saw was Lil D from the first floor.

"Shanna, where you been? You jus' disappeared!"

"Nobody told you what happen?" I asked Lil D.

"I heard you had to move wit' yo' aunt because you was having problems at school."

"Hell naw."

"What happen then?"

"I wanted to move, so I did. Where is Carl, Lil D? I ain't seen him in a long time."

"Check in da alley, he probly playin' ball."

Lil D walked me to the alley where they shot hoops. I saw a few of my friends in the back playing basketball, but I didn't see Carl. I asked everybody had they seen Carl, and they said that he usually was around, so I shot a couple hoops and waited.

"Shanna, we have to go. It's getting dark, and you know how Ms. Rolland is." Altavese looked at her watch.

I was thinking, fuck you, I want to see my brother, but I knew she was right. On the ride back home, I didn't say a word because I went on a blank mission. I missed my brother, and I wanted to get real high - real fast. When we got back to the attic, I had homework to do, but I didn't do it. I sat in front of the TV and didn't really watch it. I just sat.

When I went back to school, I started smoking more weed, and I started drinking too. Old English and Wild Irish Rose were the popular drinks. I fell behind again in my schoolwork, and I started getting high before I went to school, so I slept in class.

I just didn't give a damn anymore because I felt let down, and I knew that I wouldn't see my brother again. I stopped coming home from school, and Ms. Rolland started talking to me about my behavior and God's plan for my life.

I was back to being messed up, and it only took a week.

"What's going on wit' you? You was doing good." Ms. Rolland asked.

"I'm okay."

"No, you not, Shanna, your weekend visit with yo' Mother is coming up, should I tell her you're coming or what?"

"You can tell her what you want, I don't care."

"Naw, you need to go for the weekend cuz I don't want to deal wit' you. I'm fed up."

My mother couldn't pick me up, so Altavese told me which buses to catch. I got to my Mom's house, well her hotel room, in less than an hour. She was closer to me closer than Carl.

I was mad at my momma too. I just dropped down on her bed.

"You tired huh," Lester, momma's friend, asked. I didn't answer. "You sure are pretty. Clare, you sure she is you daughter," he laughed.

"Yea, she's my daughter, but she looks more like her father. He's Irish!"

I looked at my mother and said, "I thought my daddy was Puerto Rican."

"Who told you that? That bitch Beth told you that shit, didn't she?" Momma asked.

"Yeah."

"I hate what that bitch did to me. She took my kids."

My mom started talking about how Beth took Carl and me away from her. The story she told was different than what I remembered. Her version didn't include her leaving me and Carl hungry and alone. She was pissing me off, but thank God, Lester fired up a joint and helped me to leave the past in the past.

"How you doing in school, Shanna?" He asked.

"I'm doing good," I lied.

I could have been doing good, but I wasn't. I managed to get by. Even high, I realized being over at my mother's wasn't much different than being at Ms. Rolland's or Beth's. The only places that were different was school and hanging out.

Learning stuff was different and being with my friends was different. Momma's place, Beth's place, and Ms. Rolland's place were all the same; they all made me sad. I liked being at school. My friends were at school, and at school I wasn't sad. Lester passed me the joint again. I hit it again realizing that I wanted to be around my friends.

My popularity at school was getting huge. I hit the joint again, school and my friends were real . . . everything else was sad and phony, including my momma. I passed her the joint. It was sad to make that realization, considering what day it was.

CHAPTER 12

Mother's Love

It was Mother's Day, and I felt compelled to buy my mother something. I wanted to surprise my mother with the gifts I bought her so, I left the gifts in my bag.

After we smoked the weed and drank a couple of drinks, I gave my mother her gifts, a rose and a Mother's Day certificate.

"Happy Mother's Day Mom!"

My Mom took the gifts and started to cry with tears of joy.

"Look Lester, Shanna bought me this for Mother's Day!"

"That's nice of you Shanna, you made yo Mother happy!"

I didn't think anything of gifts, but I must admit when my mother hung the certificate on her dresser mirror, I felt I did something right for a change.

Lester never said much to me, but since I did something that made my Mother happy, he began to talk more. Later, my Mom had to go somewhere and she said that she'll be right back, so Lester and I stayed in the room. Lester rolled some more weed and we talked about how happy my mother was when I gave her the gifts.

"Lester, can I go to see Randall and tell him hello?"

My mom had a friend down the hall named Randall who I had gotten cool with over the visits. He was a drunk, and all the other drunks hung-out over his place, but he always treated me nice and I liked him.

"Yes, try to make it back befo' yo' momma get back!"

"Okay."

I went a few doors down and knocked on Randall's door.

"Heyyyy, its Clare's daughter."

"Come on in!" The alcoholics welcomed me in.

"What y'all drinking?" I asked.

"You don't want none of this stuff!"

"What is it? I can handle it."

"Ten High, this shit right here get you fucked up!"

I poured a tall cup full of the cheap drink and guzzled it down.

"Whoa! Whoa!" Randall said while holding his hand up.

"I'm fine."

It seemed like everybody in the room got quiet because they knew I had drunk too much in a short amount of time. Slowly, I felt the drink creeping up on me then I sat down and watched the room spin from slow to fast. The music became a strange sound to my ears and faces became distorted and all of a sudden…black. I had to be carried out by God knows who, and when I woke up all I heard was my mother yelling at me and I wasn't fully awake.

I was laying on the floor, and when I tried to get up, I threw up.

"Yo' ass think you grown, don't ya, that's what yo' ass get. What happened, Lester?" Mother yelled.

"She got drunk wit yo' friends down the hall."

"Tell me the truth Lester. Were y'all fucking while I was gone?"

"What!"

I had to second that emotion.

"What? I don't want to have sex wit' him!" I slurred.

"Shut the fuck up, I ain't talking to you! Did you, Lester?"

Lester kept explaining to my mother what really happened.

Apparently, she didn't believe either of us. I threw up so much that the bucket Lester had given me was full, and I had to carry it down the hall and empty it in the toilet. Every time I threw up, the color would change. At first it was purple and then pink.

"Shanna, I want you to get out of my house because I can't trust you around my man wit' yo' hot ass!"

"Can I leave later because I don't feel good?" I pleaded.

"You should have thought about that shit when you decided to be grown."

My Mother was in my face and ready to fight me. She pushed me. I pushed her back. We wrestled throughout her room then my mother pinned me down on the floor.

"I know you fucked my man because yo' fast ass is always in his face. I told yo' nasty attitude having ass not to fuck wit' me!"

Lester pulled my mother up off me, and I immediately pulled the certificate off of her mirror, stomped the rose, told my mother that she wasn't my mother, and that I hated her.

"I ain't yo mother, huh!"

Then my mother motioned to hit me, and Lester grabbed her and told me to go home, so I did.

I was drunk and walked to the bus stop throwing up. By the time I got on the el' train, the vomit had turned clear. I had thrown up all I had inside.

As soon as I walked in the door, "Shanna, yo' mother called and she told me what happened and look at you, you look a mess," Ms. Rolland said while scratching her wig.

I went upstairs to my bed and slept all the next day. Later that evening, Ms. Rolland wanted to know what happened.

"Shanna, I got to know what happened at yo' mother's house, and look at your face, it's scratched up."

"You know what happened because my mother told you."

I put the pillow on top of my head.

"I thought that getting you and yo' mother together would be a good thing, but now I have to report this. Your mother was trying to be a good mother, but now you messed that up. I don't know what is going to happen with you, it's out of my hands."

I kept going to school because it was almost graduation time, and I was a little excited about that. I continued to hang out with my friends, Stan and Nadia, until Stan started becoming interested in me, as if I was his girlfriend. I had never taken him seriously because he had gay tendencies, and everybody knew it except him. Stan asked me would I be his girlfriend, and I said no and laughed at him. I didn't want to jeopardize our friendship because he was confused. After I said no, Stan turned on me.

We were at our eighth grade luncheon, and everybody looked so good, including me, and I couldn't believe that Ms. Rolland bought me a new outfit for the occasion. I had on a long white blouse with black pants, looking really nice.

Stan looked handsome too with his maroon two-piece suit. We were waiting for our teacher to give us our nametags for the luncheon, and she finally called me. I went up to get my nametag and then I heard everybody giggle under their breath. When I got up again the giggles became laughs.

"What is everybody laughing for?" I asked out loud.

"Look on the back of yo' shirt, mommy!" One of the Hispanic boys said.

I looked, and it was blue ink and chewed bubble gum on my new white shirt, and I immediately looked at Stan. He had looked up to the ceiling as if God was calling him.

"You gay bitch, you wish you can have me or look like me, which one is it, Stan?"

Nydia got in between the two of us and calmed everybody down.

"We are friends, y'all need to talk or som'in," was Nydia's attempt for peace.

I tried to get the gum and ink off my shirt the best I could, so I got creative and tied the shirt where the stain was, which made the shirt look better. I know Stan thought that he had ruined my day, but he lost.

The day of the graduation came, and I was excited and happy to put on my cap and gown . . . blue and gold! Nydia, another girl, and me smoked a joint before we marched down the aisle. We were laughing through the whole ceremony.

After the graduation, we took pictures and signed each other's books. Everybody in the house came to my graduation, which surprised me. I looked for my mother but didn't see her.

When we all got home there was a package for me, it was from my mother. I opened the box, and it was a boom box and a card with some money. I wanted my mother to come to my graduation, but I had become immune to her absence. A couple of days later, Ms. Rolland called me to her bedroom, and I knew what she wanted.

"I think you know what I'm gonna tell you, right?"

"Yeah, I know."

"I wanted to wait until you at least graduated befo' I spring this on you. I tried to work wit' you, but nothing was working. I hope you can find a place you like, and may God bless you!"

I wanted to tell Ms. Rolland to shut the hell up, but I stood in her room listening to her lie about how she wished I would find happiness.

"Bring all yo' clothes down, so I can wash them because you are leavin' Monday."

I felt a little melancholy, but I knew that I would have to leave, so I packed my clothes and my feelings.

CHAPTER 13

The Haunted Mansion (A Group Home)

I asked the worker who was driving, "Where am I'm going?"
She answered, "A place on the Westside," but she didn't say what type of place.

All I heard was, "Westside," and I started thinking about Carl. I assumed she was driving me to another home; I assumed wrong. When we arrived at the place, I looked and looked again because we were at a haunted mansion. It was surrounded by a brick wall and gloomy bent over trees. I was expecting lightening, bats, and black cats.

"What is this place?"

"This is a group home for young girls such as yourself; you'll make lots of friends here."

The place didn't feel friendly to me. We had to walk through metal double doors and staff to get in. The place felt like a jail or prison. The worker didn't hand my papers to a foster mother; she slid them through a glass partition to a worker behind the glass. She sat with me in the office area while my paper work was being processed.

"Am I at Juvy?"

"No, this is a group home. You will like it, wait and see."

She didn't look at me once while she said I would like it. Her words didn't stop my worry. When my paper work was finished, a big manly looking lady came and escorted me through more double doors. The worker didn't follow us. I was alone. I really felt like an inmate as I followed behind the manly woman.

The place was noisy with girl chatter, and it smelled like a school or doctor's office. I could tell by the noise and the groups of girls that a lot went on. The manly looking lady opened the room door, and there were five beds in this room, five flat beds. The walls were lime green and white. The manly woman pointed to unmade bed with sheets and a blanket folded at the foot. I went to it, and she left.

I sat, and sat some more. I didn't see this type of place coming because I knew nothing about group homes. That was the first time in a long time that I cried.

I heard a loud ass voice on the intercom announcing activities time. I heard a knock on the door, but I refused to answer it. I was wallowing in tears and didn't want to be bothered. The door opened, and the noise of the place came in with a lady that had on a counselor's nametag.

"Shashanna, that is yo' name, right? Do you want to participate in the activities? We are playing checkers and spades."

"No," I buried my faced in the flat pillow.

"Well, you gonna have to meet your roommates sooner or later, why not now?"

"No, I don't want to!" I yelled into the pillow.

I didn't want to meet my roommates. I just wanted to leave. The room got quiet, so I guessed she left. I had fallen asleep but woke up when a couple of girls came into the room and started talking to me.

"We gone have dinner, so you gone have to come out. Roz, that big lady that brought you back here, is gonna make you come out. My name is Candy, and this is Tanya, Jennie, and Lavone is in the TV room. We sleep in here too. What's yo' name?"

I didn't answer Candy because I didn't want to sound like I had been crying.

I was clearing my throat when she said, "Well fuck you then, we is trying to be nice to yo' ass and shit!"

The door slammed, and I started crying again.

A few minutes later, I heard a knock, "Can I come in?" I didn't answer, but the manly looking woman came in anyway. Standing in the doorway with the door open she said, "I know you upset, but you gonna have to come out and get to know everybody here. Face it, this is where you live now, so get used to it. It might not be home, but it's not so bad here. If something goes wrong around here, I'm the person that keeps things in check. I'm Roz and don't be scared to talk to me."

I sat up, wiping the tears from my face. I was through crying. She was right, where I was . . . was where I was. I had to deal with it.

"You never been to a group home before have you?" Roz asked with sincerity. I shook my head no. I guess she thought I had left my "real home" with my natural mother. "Come on and get something to eat, I know you hungry. I ain't gone lie, some of these girls you have to watch out for because they get jealous of pretty girls like you, and if that happens, tell me." Roz said while tapping her chest with her fist.

Roz made me feel secure enough to come out of the room to eat and meet the other girls.

When I got to the lunch room I felt eyes staring at me. I didn't know who to sit by or who to talk to. But what I did know was that I would have to fight in that place. I felt the eyes and the tension.

"You po-ta-Rican or something?" One girl blurted.

I looked over at her, "No," I answered.

"What's yo' name?" An older looking girl asked.

"What's yo' name?" I asked with attitude.

"I'm Terri." The skinny older girl said.

"Shanna." I said with no attitude.

I sat down and tried to eat the crap that was on the tray, but I couldn't do it.

"After y'all eat, go straight to the TV room!" Roz snapped out.

I went to the TV room as ordered. There were girls looking at videos, which I loved. I sat on the sagging couch and watched "Thriller." A couple of girls sat by me, and one touched my hair.

"Is this yo' hair?"

"Yeah," I answered still watching "Thriller."

I was used to black folks thinking my hair was special. Then a girl pulled my hair, hard.

I turned my head to face her, "What chu doing?"

"I don't think I like yo' yellow ass!"

The girl's face was drawn in tight like a squirrel, and it was marked with old scars.

"Leave that girl alone; don't be jealous," Terri, the older girl from the lunchroom, said, stepping into the TV room.

"I ain't jealous of huh. I jus' don't like huh!" The ugly girl said, standing up from the couch and crossing her arms.

I thought it was fight time, so I stood up too. I didn't want to be at a disadvantage. Then Terri pulled me away from the TV and the ugly squirrel looking girl. I didn't like her pulling me, but I didn't know who was cool and who wasn't, and I didn't feel like fighting. So I went with her to the other side of the TV room.

"You was ready to fight wasn't you?" She smiled at me. I didn't answer. "Yeah well, Candy likes to fight so be careful. She is your roommate, and your other two roommates, Tanya and Jennie, follow behind her like they ain't got brains of they own, so again, be careful."

"Ok," was all I said because I didn't trust her or them.

"Where you from, Shashanna?"

"Westside."

"Where on the Westside?"

"Adams and St. Louis."

"Áwwh shit, I got family ova there, you know Wanda and Lil D?"

"Yeah!"

"Awh man, I know we gonna be cool."

I felt a little better since she knew people I knew. We smiled at each other, but I didn't feel like talking, so I told her I'd see her later and went to my room and unpacked my clothes and put them in the assigned dresser drawers.

Candy, the ugly squirrel girl, came in, and we just stared each other down then she left. Tanya and Jennie came in to get a couple of things out of their drawers and stared at me briefly and left. I spent my first day at the group home laying in my bed, wishing I was someplace else.

When it was time to go to bed, Candy, Tanya, Jennie, and Lavone came into the room and got ready for bed. They pulled off their clothes in front of each other, which made me think they were gay.

Lavone looked over me and asked, "Is you nervous? It's ok if you is. I was nervous too at first, but you will get use to everybody like we all did."

"Fuck huh, she think she is betta than us because she is white!" Candy blurted out.

I didn't even look her way.

"Leave that girl alone, Candy. You play too much," Lavone said, getting into her bed.

They started talking to each other, so I relaxed a bit. They kept talking, even after they were in bed. When the lights went out, I thought it was going to get quiet, but they kept on. I covered my head with my pillow and blanket to fall asleep.

It seemed like only minutes passed before the intercom woke me announcing breakfast and morning meeting. I was late for everything that first day.

"Shashanna, since you is new around here, I'm gonna let you slide, but tomorrow you gonna have to get up when I say you get up." Roz sternly said while twirling her keys on her hip.

"Roz, why we have to get up so early; school is over?" I asked.

"Those are the rules around here, either you get up on time or get points off of your weekend pass."

"Weekend pass, what's that?"

"You get to go home to an adult and stay the weekend away from this place."

Those words sounded like music and motivation. I was up the next morning and the mornings that followed. I fell into the routine of the place, hoping for that pass, not knowing who I was going to see or where I was going. I got cool with Terri, who was the oldest girl in the group home, and she got her respect.

One day she asked me, "Do you smoke weed? If you do I know where to get some around here, but I have to get it when we get a pass to go to the store."

"Cool," I answered very interested but trying not to get too excited.

"When I go to the store today, I'm gonna ask Roz can you go wit' me, ok?"

"Okay."

"This guy I know sells joints for a dolla a piece. We get five dollars a week around here, and we can put our money together if we want a bag, what chu think?"

"Hell yeah."

Weed came to my rescue at that group home. I settled down-and-in once me and Terri started getting high. The daily routine went smoother high, and I got better at getting along. But my roommates were still weird, and I felt the pressure of their attitudes every day.

The derogatory statements from Candy where always present. She wanted a fight, but I was always cool around her; the weed helped. Words that would have caused me to snap off before the group home barely upset me. I was thinking about the pass and Candy's advice to stay cool. I was dealing with the other kids pretty good, but the betrayal that got me came from an adult.

I was in the TV room and Roz asked, "Shanna, you have some lotion for my ashy hands? I thought I had some in my purse, but I must have left it at home."

"Yeah, I have some, I'll be right back."

I didn't think twice about getting Roz some lotion because I felt she was looking out for me, and it was an honor to do her a favor. When I got to my room, Candy, Tanya and Jennie were waiting on me. Tanya blocked the door, and Candy pushed me on my bed and jumped on top of me.

"Bitch, you had this coming; we finna beat yo' ass!"

And they did, I got a couple good punches in but not many. Finally, Roz came in the room acting like she wasn't aware of what was happening.

"What the fuck is y'all doing to that girl?"

They didn't immediately jump off of me. They slapped me a couple of more times with her in the room. She knew what was happening to me. When they got off of me, I walked past her without a word. The bitch was part of the set up, and I knew it.

I was in the bathroom at a sink, running cold water into my hands and rinsing my face. Ugly girls always attacked my face. When I looked in the mirror, I flinched. The bruises were already starting to show. My eyes were turning black and swelling. Terri busted into the bathroom.

"Shanna, I heard that Candy and them jumped you in y'all room. Let me see yo' face." I dropped my hands. "Damn!"

She pulled out a bunch of paper towels and wet them and pressed them against my face.

"Stay here."

She came back with ice and towels and made me sit on the bathroom floor while she pressed the towels and ice to my face.

"Yo' face is fucked up with scratches and bruises. I know you wanna get them back."

I did, but I noticed she did not say "we" could get them back. A group jumped on me, but I didn't have a group. And I didn't just want revenge on the girls, I wanted revenge on Roz's manly looking ass too. I knew that if Roz knew how I felt, she had the power to take my privileges away, and she could let Candy and the others beat me up again. I let the days pass and my wounds heal while revenge festered in my mind.

One day Terri and I went to the store, and I had on a red hat. This guy approached me and snatched my hat off and stomped it.

"What the fuck you do that for, pick my hat up!"

"Bitch, what you ride?"

The boy got in my face.

"The bus," I responded sarcastically.

"Shanna, he means what gang is you in," Terry laughed nervously.

"I ain't in no gang, so what my red hat got to do wit' that?"

"Bitch, that's a Vice lord hat, we GD's around here!"

I remembered the Vice Lord's colors being black and gold, but never red, so this was news to me.

"Will you give me my hat?" I said with my arm reaching.

"Shanna, don't get into it wit' them because I can't help you if something jump off," Terri said.

I looked at the guy then I looked at Terri, and I picked my own hat up off the ground.

"Don't wear that hat around here no mo'!" The thug said.

I decided Terri was no real help, and that clear thought made me like her less.

Back at the prison, the rumor spread that Candy and her girls were planning to jump me again, and I wasn't about to get beat up twice. I went straight to our room and found Candy alone and taking a nap.

I jumped her while she was sleeping. My punches were all hard and all straight to the head. Even after she stopped fighting back, I continued to throw blows. I was grabbed from the back and thrown off of her and to the floor. It was Roz. I got to my feet quick and squared off in front of her.

"What's wrong with you, girl?"

I didn't answer her. She moved her eyes from me to Candy then she picked Candy up and carried her out of the room without saying another word to me. Nobody slept in the room with me that night. In the morning, Roz came into the room.

"All your passes, gone, and ya ass is confined to the room with no privileges.

"I don't give a fuck; I don't have nowhere to go anyway."

My roommates returned to the room, but only Lavone talked to me.

"You the only one that ever whipped Candy's ass." She said.

"I was sleep." Candy screamed.

"You ain't now," I said.

She dropped her eyes from me, stripped off her clothes, and got her ugly ass in the bed. No talking that night, but I stayed awake until I heard them all breathing heavy.

About two days later, Terri came to my room and whispered, "Shashanna, I am running away. If you down I'll let you know when. You down?"

"Hell yeah," I said and meant it.

Candy's confidence was building as her wounds healed, and she and her girls were starting to stare me down again.

Sunday morning came, and Terri walked past my door and mouthed, "Today."

I knew we were on, so I put on double clothes: two shirts, two pants, two bras, two of everything. After everyone ate breakfast and went to the TV room, I was to go back to my room. When I stepped into the room, Terri was already there.

"You got some clothes, Shanna?"

"Yeah, under these."

"Good. I had my boys to unscrew the bars to yo' window, and all we have to do is open the window and push the bars open."

And it was just that easy, we hit the ground running. Terri knew what busses and el train to catch to the Westside.

On the train she said, "You can stay with me at my aunt's if you can't find your brother, but at night you have to act like you leaving, but I will sneak you back in after my aunt goes to sleep."

I didn't care what she was talking about. I was about to see my brother. I was so happy to be on that train.

When the conductor said, "Laramie, Laramie is next," I almost cried.

When we got off the train, Lil D was waiting at the bottom of the steps.

"What's up Cuz, oh hell naw, you didn't tell me you had Shanna with you."

He hugged me before he hugged Terri.

"Where you been, I heard you moved to yo' antie house."

"Who told yo' that?"

"Beth."

"Naw, I was in the same group home as Terri. Hey, you seen Carl?"

"Carl stay across the bridge on Douglas, you want the address?"

"Boy, yeah!"

CHAPTER 14

My Search Is Over

I didn't mean to be rude, but as soon as he gave me the address I left them. It had been two years since I saw my brother. I made it to the address; it was a court-way building. I ran up the stairs to the number Lil' D told me and knocked on the door. There was a security gate across the door. A lady opened the door.

"Is Carl here?" I asked.

"Who is you?"

"I'm his susta, Shanna."

"Oh yeah, I heard a lot about you, I'm Carl's girlfriend; let me get the lock off this gate. Carl!"

By time she got the locks off the gate, Carl was standing behind her, and he pulled the gate open for me.

We hugged long and hard. At that point, I became overjoyed and forgot about my current situation. I couldn't believe that my journey was over, and that I was looking at my brother.

"Baby sis, baby sis, baby sis."

I didn't want to cry, but the tears came anyway. When we let go of each other, we both quickly wiped the tears from our faces.

We smiled, and he said, "This is my girl, Sandra. This is my baby sis I been telling you about."

"I heard a lot about chu, Shanna. Nice to meet chu."

"Nice to meet you too," I replied.

"I been lookin' fo' you, nobody told you?" I said to Carl.

"Yeah, I heard you came around the house a couple a months ago."

"Yeah, Beth said you didn't live wit' huh anymo'!"

"That bitch didn't tell me you came. Lil D and dem told me. Girl, I'm so glad to see you."

He hugged me again.

Carl's girlfriend brought a newborn baby out and showed her to me.

"Who is this?"

Carl had a son by another girl before we separated, so I knew it wasn't the same baby.

"This is my baby girl," Carl said while simultaneously giving me the infant. "I named huh afta me and you, Ca'shanna!"

I was moved by the thought that Carl was thinking of me when his baby was born. I held Ca'shanna and gently pulled back the wrapped receiving blanket from over her face. She was beautiful.

I quickly gave her back to Carl. I didn't want to drop her.

"Where you stay at, Shanna? Beth wouldn't give me yo' number where you live."

"I live close, ova here now."

"What's tha address?"

"I can't give it to you cuz they don't want people at they house, and I'm not gonna stay long anyway."

He looked at me hard. He was hurt. I guessed he thought it was by choice that I didn't give him the address. I didn't tell Carl about running away from the group home and staying with Terri's aunt because I knew he would offer his place, at least I hoped he would, but I didn't want to stay with him. I didn't know why I didn't; I just knew I didn't.

"As long I see you now, damn girl you getting big," Carl said with joy.

He was happy to see me too.

"How long you and Sandra been together, Carl?"

"We been together a year and a half."

He was happy when he said it. I could tell he liked her a lot. All of a sudden, I heard a knock on the door; Carl went. He gave the person something, and the person gave Carl money. I understood why the door had a gate and so many locks. My brother was selling something. I didn't ask, and he didn't tell me.

"Shanna, you need some money?"

"Yeah!"

Carl gave me ten one dollar bills, which was cool because I was flat broke. I never told Carl that I was on the run because I didn't want him to worry about me. I stayed over until the street lights came on then I told Carl and Sandra that I had to go.

"Am I gonna see you again, Shanna?"

"Yeah, I'll be back in a few days."

"Okay, I love you girl."

"I love you too."

I hated not letting Carl know what was going on with me, but that was where my head was. I developed a lot of false pride.

When I got the address Terri gave me, no one answered the door. I rang the bell and knocked on the door. I went back three times and still no answer. I had nowhere to go. I walked to the park and sat on a bench. I didn't sit long. I walked to the train station and reversed the route back to the group home. I knew how to get to my bother; the group home didn't seem so bad. It was better than the park. When I got to the group home, Roz answered the door.

"What you want, you don't live here anymore."

"I came to get my clothes."

I wasn't going to admit that I was defeated, so I used my clothes as an excuse to come back. Roz was still talking to me through the closed door.

"We made a police report on you, and you are considered missing."

"Let me in, so that I can get my clothes."

"I shouldn't let your ass in because you ran away, which means that you don't want to be here."

Roz opened the door, and I stepped into the hall. Roz gave me the permission to go to my room and get my clothes. Most of my things were missing, but they didn't take the boom box Momma gave me for graduation.

"I contacted your worker. Somebody is coming to get you."

CHAPTER 15

Around The Way Girl (getting higher)

On the drive to the new placement, I saw row houses; buildings with no spaces between them. I didn't know what to expect, a facility or a home. The worker parked in front of one of the row houses. She hadn't told me if it was temporary site or a home placement. We hadn't talked at all during the long ride.

Her first words were, "I think you will like it here."

Since she didn't say temporary, I figured I was going someplace to stay for a while. There was no porch, only a couple of steps. The worker knocked on the door because there was no doorbell. A fat lady answered the door, and I smelled her before I saw her.

"Hi, come on in," the heavy lady greeted me and the worker while opening her screen door.

Once we got inside the worker said, "This is Shashanna, who is about to turn fifteen, and she is entering high school."

"It nice to meet you and have a seat right there," she pointed to an armchair next to a lamp.

I sat, and the two of them walked towards the back of the place.

They didn't talk long. The worker walked past me setting my garbage bag of belongings and boom-box on the chair; she quickly nodded her head, waved goodbye, and left.

She did say something that made me smile though; I was about to start high school.

"Come on, let's go upstairs. I am Mrs. Landers. I didn't hear the worker tell me you my name."

Walking behind her up stairs, her body odor was even stronger; I held my breath during the climb. When we got upstairs, I saw a pink girly room with four beds, bunk beds.

"Which bed you want to sleep in?" Mrs. Landers asked while fanning herself. I liked having a choice. "You can pick from three out of the four because Patricia sleeps in that bed." She said, pointing to across the room.

I decided to take the bottom bunk and began unpacking my clothes.

"Ok, I'ma let you settle in, the dresser by the window is yours."

I stayed upstairs on my lower bunk and listened to my radio. Later, Mrs. Landers called me downstairs to meet her daughter Patricia.

"Shashanna, am I sayin' it right?"

"Yes."

"Shashanna, this is my daughter, Patricia. Patricia, this is Shashanna!"

"Hi," I said.

Patricia gave me a mean look to let me know she didn't like me. Her Jeri-curl was short, and she was cockeyed.

"Shashanna, don't pay huh no mind. Patricia graduated from the school you gonna go to. Now she is in huh first year in college."

First year of college and still stupid was my thought, but the place with a fat smelly lady, and an ugly daughter was better than the "haunted mansion" for girls.

Mrs. Landers had a husband who stayed downstairs, so I hardly saw him, and two spoiled grandkids. There wasn't much going on in the house, which was cool with me. I was tired of constant drama. After a day or so, I became familiar with everyone in the house and then I ventured outside.

I wandered around to get a feel for the neighborhood. There was a field house across the street from the row houses and a store on the corner. I walked in circles because the area was a neighborhood with townhouses that were built in a circle.

I went back to the house, and Mrs. Landers asked me how I liked the neighborhood.

"I liked the open area that was across the street."

"Oh, that's Gately Stadium where they play football. Did you look across the street from the stadium?"

"No."

"The school you is going to is ova there. Later you can walk ova there and see for yo'self. All the kids around here goes to that school, so you gonna make a lot of friends."

After a week or so, the tension lessened between Patricia and me. I guessed from me walking through the neighborhood, a couple of guys must have asked her about me, so Patricia introduced me to some of her friends. One in particular was this nerdy looking guy named Dexter.

"Shanna, this is my friend, Dexter. Dexter, this is Shanna, my mom's new girl."

We were standing in front of his row house.

"New girl huh?" Dexter had that horny toad boy look in his eyes."Hi Shanna, how long have you been around here?"

"A couple of weeks."

"Would y'all like to come in?"

"Should we?" I asked Patricia.

"You never invited me in yo' house befo'" Patricia snipped.

"You can come in too, Patricia." The nerd said.

We went in the house and straight to the basement. There was a bar, which had something covered on it. Dexter saw me looking at the covers.

"Under those covers are my babies; two turn tables, and an equalizer."

"You a DJ?" I got excited.

"Yep."

"Can I see them?"

"What chu know about DJin'?"

"I know a lot. I know how to scratch and mix. My friend from Chicago Heights taught me."

I saw his crates of albums at the end of the bar and went to them.

"Fo' real, you have, "Let The Music Play"?"

He had two copies of each album.

"You know it."

"Yeah, I told you I can do this."

He put both records on the two turn tables and trusted me to touch his babies. I scratched the two records and blended the two beats together using the equalizer.

"You know a lil' something, but let me show you how it's really done."

He knew his craft, and I knew I had a friend.

"We got to go, Shanna," Patricia whined.

I forgot she was with us.

"Well, you know where I am at if you want to come back later, Shanna."

We smiled at each other.

When we got outside, I could tell that Patricia wanted to tell me something about Dexter, but she waited until we got in front of the house.

"Can't you tell he's gay? I don't know why he is actin' like he like you and everythang!"

"If he is gay, why he asked me to come ova layta?" I asked with my hands on my hips.

"I don't know. Are you going?" Patricia said while trying to roll her cocked eyes.

"Yeah."

Later, I went over to Dexter's house, but I had a hard time finding my way because every house looked the same, but eventually I got there. I rang Dexter's doorbell and a thick girl with glasses answered the door.

"Whowizzit?"

"Shanna, is Dexter here?"

"Dexter, somebody at da door for you," The thick girl yelled.

"Oh, hey, come on in."

"This is my sister, Rhonda; this is Shanna, my new friend."

"Whud!" Rhonda was in disbelief.

We went downstairs to Dexter's basement and played music and talked.

"Shanna, I think you are so pretty, do you have a boyfriend?"

"No, why?"

"Awh, I'm jus' askin'. Let me show you somemo' records. What you know about this?" Dexter boasted.

"Awh man, "Thousand Finger Man"! Thou...sand...fin...ger maaaaaaaaan!" I had to sing it to let Dexter know that I knew the song.

"You want to make a mix tape right now, since you know a little about mixing?"

I became nervous because no one had ever let me work their equipment.

"You foreal?"

"Yeah, I got a blank tape; you can mix what you want."

I didn't know where to start so, I started with my favorite song, "Let the Music Play." Every now and then I found Dexter starring at me, and I would blush and keep mixing.

"Can I call you Dex?"

"Why, you don't like my name or sumthin'?"

"Yea, but I wanna call you Dex."

"Okay, girl."

"Dex, My birthday is coming up, what we gonna do?" I asked.

"When is yo' Birthday?"

"In a couple of weeks."

"Okay."

"Do you smoke weed?" I asked.

"Naw, and you shouldn't either."

That was a strike against him, but we shared a common interest in music that would keep us friends but not best friends. As I got familiar with the neighborhood, I eventually found people who smoked weed.

This girl named Pam was first. She was wild and loose and looked mean as hell with a big head and a short body. I was at the corner store when I met her.

"Yo' name is Shanna right?" Pam asked loudly.

"Yeah, how do you know?"

"Dex's sister go to school wit' me, and she told me about you. You stay wit' Patricia and them don't chu?"

"Yeah, I know you know where some weed at, do'nt chu?" I asked while looking at Pam's oversized head.

"Hell yeah, and you know it."

Pam had her hands on her small framed body. Pam took me to this house, and an older guy answered the door.

"Tony, this is Shanna, she wants some weed."

"Can she speak fo' huhself?"

"Do you sell joints?" I asked.

Tony was a heavy older guy with a Jerri Curl.

"No, but fuh you, I'll give you some weed. Wait right here."

While Pam and I waited for Tony to bring some joints we talked.

"Damn girl, he don't do shit like that. So, where you from?"

"The Westside."

"Oh, I heard about that side of town. What school you go to, Shanna?"

"I'm supposed to go to da high school by that stadium."

"My dad is da gym teacher ova there; I go to a all-girl school."

Tony came back to the door and told me to open my hands. He filled them with weed.

"Thank you!"

I was too happy because I thought I was only getting a joint or two.

"When you need some more, come back, and don't bring huh wit' you." He nodded his head towards Pam.

"Shut up Tony, he jus' playin'." Pam disregard Tony's bold request.

Pam and I went to the corner store to get some rolling papers and a paper bag to put the weed in.

"This should last me until my birthday." I announced.

"When is yo' birthday, Shanna?"

"Next week!"

"Hell yeah, we gonna get fucked up fo' yo' Birthday!" Pam was too hyped.

After that day, Pam and I started hanging out every day, drinking and getting high. We were walking through the neighborhood and saw this guy with a lot of girls on his porch. He called out to me.

"Hey girl, come here."

I looked at Pam and she said, "That's Rich old ass thinking he a playa and shit. Come on, let's see what he wants."

We walked over to his porch. Rich started a conversation with me as if no one else was around.

"Don't you live wit' Patricia and them?" The guy asked me.

"Yeah, why?" I snapped.

"I been watchin' you girl, that's why."

"You a playa or sumthin'?"

"Naw, I ain't even like that. Pam, you told huh that?"

Pam turned her head away.

"Come here, come closah!"
"What, you want to kiss me or sumthin'." I said
"You want me to? Foreal tho, my name is Rich. What's yo' name?"
"Shanna, but I think you know that already."
"You right, I know yo' name," Rich smiled
"How old are you, Rich?"
"I'm twenty-two, do it matta?"
"Naw, I'm jus' askin'"
Rich's age didn't bother me at all.
"How old are you?" He asked me.
"I'll be fifteen in a couple of days."
"You a young buck."
"And…"

While Rich was talking, I swear his smile never left his face. Right then, I learned that being attractive was more than a pretty face because Rich wasn't pretty. I think Rich liked my swagger, and I liked his too. We talked for a while on his porch, and the other girls and Pam left us alone.

"You smoke weed?" Rich smiled again.
"Yeah, I have some on me. You want to smoke a joint?" I reached for the weed Tony had given me.
"That's what I'm sayin', fi' it up!"

Rich was so funny, he had me laughing the whole time that we were together, and I didn't want that night to end.

"I got to get ready to go because my curfew is at nine o'clock."
"When I'm gonna see you again, Shanna?"
"Maybe tomorrow." I said flirting.
"No maybe, I'm gonna see you tomorrow." Rich said as if he was in charge of us seeing each other again.

"We'll see."

As I walked away, I felt Rich watching me, so I turned around to catch him, and kept walking.

I didn't even get to walk in the house good before Patricia's cockeyed butt was in my face.

"I saw you ova there on Rich's porch, what was y'all talkin' about?"

"Nothing."

"You know he is older than you, right?"

"I know Patricia, damn."

"He got a lot of women; you should be careful because his girls might get mad and beat you up."

"I ain't worried about no girls beating me up."

"Okay."

I woke up the next morning with a smile; I wanted to see Rich. I showered, dressed, washed the dishes, and hit the door in less than hour.

When I rang Rich's doorbell this mean ass sounding lady answered the door, "What do you want?"'

"Is Rich here?"

"Rich is sleep and don't come by here asking fo' him nomo."

I thought she was going to slam the door. But she stood there staring me down. I turned away quickly because I was pissed off. If that was Rich's mother, I didn't want to act a fool. I went back home and helped with the cleanup chores, but I couldn't stop thinking that Rich might be outside, so I went out.

Walking towards his house, I ran into Pam, who was waiting on me to smoke some weed with her.

"Fi' it up Shanna, I know you got somemo' of that shit!"

"Yep, I sho' do!"

I thought I would have enough weed to last for my Birthday, but I didn't. I went through it faster than I thought.

"Damn Pam, you gonna have to get me some weed."

"Uh uh, get it from yo' boyfriend!"

"What boyfriend?"

"Tony, the man who gave you all that weed!"

"You think he would give me some mo'?"

"Yeah, let's go to his house."

We went around to Tony's house, and to my surprise, he told us to come in.

"How y'all doing, sit down and role a joint!" Tony said while spraying curl activator on his hair.

He and his hair looked nasty, but the big pile of weed on the coffee table looked good. I had never seen so much weed. I became more nervous, and it must have shown.

"Don't be scared, you safe wit' me!" Tony said.

"I ain't scared."

"Yeah, ok. Shanna, you want a beer to relax?"

"Um Tony, I'm here too." Pam said while waving her hand in the air.

"You can get yo' own beer."

"No thanks." I said.

"You shy or something. Loosen up girl."

After we smoked a joint or two, I did loosen up, "Tony, how long you been selling weed?"

"I really don't sell weed to everybody, only my friends."

I didn't believe him, but I was high and really didn't care if he lied. I was looking at two big black plastic bags in the corner, and he saw me looking.

"Go ahead, look in them." Tony insisted.

I looked in the two bags and they were full of weed, and I looked at Tony and said, "Damn!"

I never seen so much weed. I thought that it wasn't real, so I touched and smelled it.

"Can I get some of this fo' my Birthday?"

"When is your Birthday?"

"Tomorrow."

Tony reached in the garbage bag and gave me a hand full.

"Here, Happy Birthday."

"My Birthday is coming up too," Pam's voice went up an octave.

"Get some from Shanna." Tony told her.

I had to get a zip lock bag to hold the weed that I was given, so Tony gave me one and closed it. We continued to smoke weed, and by that time I wanted a beer to boost my high.

Tony tried hard to get Pam to leave, but I gave her a look to let her know not to leave me, so she stayed.

"I think you are cute, Shanna, you have a boyfriend?"

"No, ain't you too old fuh me?"

"Not if you think age is an issue."

"You a trip!" I said with a fake laugh.

I didn't like Tony in the way he wanted me to, but I wanted more weed from him, so I played along.

"Girl, we got to go, yo' momma told you she want you to go to tha' store fuh huh, remember?" Pam was saving me.

"Damn, you right. I talk to you lata Tony, thanks."

"No problem baby, come back by yo'self, ok?"

"Okay."

When we got outside, I told Pam, "Good lookin' out."

"I know, I could tell you was ready to go." Pam confirmed.

On our way to Pam's house, we heard a horn blow.

"What's up, girl?"

I looked and saw Rich.

"Girl, you like Rich, wit' his tripped out ass. Don't ya?" Pam asked.

I couldn't hide the smile.

"Gone on wit' him, just leave me some weed."

I gave Pam some weed and got in Rich's car. Being with Rich made me feel like I had escaped from reality, he made me feel free.

"I came by yo' house earlier, but a lady told me you was sleep and not to come back no mo'."

"That's my mom, she told me you came by earlier. I tell you what; wait until she goes to work at twelve thirty, ok?"

"Twelve-thirty?"

"Yeah."

"Why you sleep so late?" I asked Rich.

"I work nights. I'm a security guard."

"Oh, that's good."

I felt safe with Rich, but I wondered about all those girls.

"What's up with these girls, I be seeing and hearing so much about?"

"Those were my sister, Roda's, friends. Roda is cool, I want you to meet huh, and she has long hair, just like you. So, why are you staying wit' Mrs. Landers?" Rich asked.

"I'm jus' living there."

My excitement quickly went away.

"Awh, you don't want to talk about it."

I knew Rich knew why I was living with Mrs. Landers.

"I know Patricia told you a lot of bad things about me, but they not true. She tried to get wit' me a long time ago, and I didn't want huh like that, so she got this chip on her shoulder."

Rich felt the need to explain his position. While Rich was pleading his case, I took some weed out and rolled a joint and fired it up.

"Damn girl, you know you be having some weed and it's good. Where you get it from?"

"Pam's friend sell weed, you have to ask huh."

We smoked weed and drove around and laughed until it was time for me to go in.

"I'm gonna drop you off because I know you have a curfew."

"I don't have to go in now." I insisted.

"Yeah, I betta get you home befo' I go to jail."

"Why you say that?"

"Duh, our age differences, and you staying wit' Mrs. Landers."

"Okay. Okay."

Rich never said that I lived in a foster home, but I knew he knew.

Before Rich dropped me off, he leaned towards me and kissed my lips. I blushed and got out of the car and went in the house.

I thought about that kiss all night long.

I woke up to my birthday and Patricia saying, "Dexter is at the door for you."

I went downstairs to the door.

"Hi Dexter, how you doing? I heard you came by yesterday."

"You haven't been over here in a while; I jus' was seeing how you was doing," Dexter's voice was calm, real matter of fact.

I guessed he was trying to sound cool.

"Me and Pam been hanging out, and I'm sorry that I haven't came ova." I exclaimed.

"I heard different, you been hanging out with Rich stupid ass haven't you?"

"Dex!"

"Naw, I don't like his ass because he is spreading rumors that I'm gay, and he makes fun of me all the time."

I felt the need to change the subject.

"Today is my Birthday!"

"Oh yeah, Happy Birthday, Shanna, I got something for you."

"What?"

"Remember that mix tape you made, here it is. I took it to the studio and put some finishing touches on it."

"Dex!"

I smiled because someone thought about me for a change, and it felt really good. I gave Dex a hug and thanked him.

A car horn honked; it was Rich.

"I got to go Shanna, Happy Birthday."

And he left.

"What's up girl? Happy Birthday."

"Thanks, you so sweet."

"Whatchu you want to do?" Rich asked.

"I want to get tow up."

"Okay, we can do that."

I felt special on my birthday because I had a boyfriend to spend it with.

For weeks, I hung out with Rich every day. Rich never made any sexual advances towards me, and that made me like him even more, but in my mind, I wanted him to be the first. I didn't count the time with Neal, because I really didn't feel nothing but being sore. I thought that Rich was worthy enough to take my virginity because he made me feel good about myself. I think Rich was nervous because I told him I was a virgin, and I was younger. He said we would know when the time was right, but he started getting jealous of everybody who spoke to me, especially Dexter.

"Why Dexter trying to push up on you, he's gay as a crowd of happy people."

"If he's gay why you worried about him? I'm not doing nothin' wit' that boy, I like you."

Rich started wanting all my time. It was fun at first, but being told by him that I had to be with him got old fast. I started not going over his house and not calling him. School was getting ready to start, high school, and I wasn't going to be going over his house all the time. I needed my space, so I stopped going to see him.

CHAPTER 16

Freshman Blues (About to Lose Myself)

I finally started high school, and walking around my new school felt good, but again, I was the new girl with no friends. I never fit into a crowd easily, but I made my own way.

The first couple of weeks, as usual, I was a loner, and I appeared different because I didn't have the designer clothes the kids wore, but what really made me different was I really didn't care about being different. My plain clothes were fine, and I was certain I would make friends. I always did.

Most of the girls at school made fun of me because of my plain clothes and the way I fixed my hair and the way I spoke. The medication for my seizures slurred my speech. I'm used to getting teased about having light skin and different hair, but not how I spoke. That teasing really hurt. My first couple weeks of high school were horrible.

I was leaving school one day feeling like a freak, an outsider, a weirdo, and Rich was parked in front of the school.

"Shanna, what's up baby, you don't know me anymo'? Come here!"

"What chu want, Rich?" I said, walking over to him.

"Cool out girl, I jus' wanna give you a ride home."

I got in the car with Rich, and it felt good seeing him because I felt like I belonged somewhere.

"You miss me, Shanna?"

"You miss me?" I asked while rolling my eyes.

"You know I do. You so mean though, and I wasn't sure if I could come up to yo' school and pick you up. Lean ova here and give me a hug."

I did, and we both laughed. When we got in front of Rich's house, he leaned over and hugged me again and tried to kiss me, but I pulled away.

"My breath stank or sumthin'?" Rick asked with a frown on his face.

"Naw, I haven't seen you in weeks, and out of nowhere you want me to kiss you?"

"Shanna, I missed you so much, I jus' wanna kiss you, can I?"

"Not now."

"I tell you what, come upstairs with me, and we can have something to drink, ok?"

"Okay, wait till I drop my book bag off at the house, and I'll be back."

"Don't take too long," Rich had urgency in his voice.

School had me lonely, so I rushed to put my book bag in the house and rushed to get back over to Rich's.

"Was that fast enough for you?" I asked him.

"Naw, you took too long, come on in."

We were sitting on his bed, and I closed his bedroom door with my foot. I really wasn't missing Rich, but with things going bad at school, at least he was somebody to talk to. I laid down on his pillow and he did too.

I didn't think he would do that, get real close to me, because he always said I wasn't ready for the real stuff. He slowly started outlining my face with his index finger, my lips, my nose, my ears, and my eyes.

"Do you know how pretty you are?"

I did, but I said, "No."

I wasn't feeling very pretty. School was always the place that made me feel better, but the teasing I was getting for taking my medicine bothered me because I had to take the medicine. The medicine was my responsibility; something I had to do for me. Being teased about it at a place I liked . . . hurt me. And it was like some kids figured it out that it really bothered me because they kept it up.

"You are though, real pretty."

Looking into his eyes on that pillow, Rick seemed ok. He kissed me, and I kissed him back.

"Let's get high."

"Cool," I said sitting up.

We drank beer and smoked weed, and he kept asking me did I miss him as much as he missed me. I said I did, but I didn't. He seemed like he missed me though, a lot. And I kind of like that. He made me feel better.

We started kissing again and I whispered, "I'm ready," in his ear.

"Ready for what?"

"You know," I looked down at my girly part.

"Shanna, you mean . . ."

"Yes."

"Are you sure, baby?"

I was, but I didn't know why. I wanted to do something special for him because he made me feel better and I was drunk and high and feeling good instead of sad, so I told him I was ready to do it.

Rich took off his shirt and then I took off mine to match his actions and then he took his pants off and I took off mine. He laid beside me and asked me again was I sure.

"Yes."

I wish I could say it was one of the most memorable moments of my life, but I cannot. I remember being nervous, but mostly I remember making the decision to give Rich my virginity because he made me feel better about the teasing I was getting at school. He made me feel better, so I wanted to make him feel better.

It was over before I knew it happened. I felt no different. I was naked. He was naked. He put his thing inside of me, but it didn't hurt or feel really good. He shivered and moaned and then rolled off of me.

"Girl, do you know how long I waited for you? I'm not finished yet."

I looked at Rich's penis, and it filled half of the condom; the rest of the condom was flat and empty. Rich got hard again, and half the condom was still hanging from his penis. We did it again and again… but still, I felt nothing really special. I was ready to leave.

"You okay, baby?" Rich asked. I got up and started putting on my clothes. "Hey, where you going so fast?"

"I have to go and do my homework because if I don't do it now, I won't get it done."

"Damn girl, you jus' don't know." He stretched out across the bed.

I didn't stop dressing. I was finished with Rich. The high was gone and so was my virginity.

Time passed, and school got better. I was getting to know some of the guys in my algebra class: Lemar, Chris, and Otis. They made algebra class fun and more interesting. Lemar became my hommie for life, Chris was on the football team, and Otis was on the Jessie White Tumbling team. We signified on each other in class and sometimes we would run out of jokes then we would talk about others, but in all the signifying they never talked about my slurred speech.

Lemar talked about Chris, Chris would talk about Lemar, I talked about both of them and they talked about me, but no one talked about Otis because he was too buffed. He observed and laughed with the class.

"Shanna, Lemar said yo' ass is white, and you don't belong in this school!" Chris yelled during a class.

Lemar had a long head and that was a target Chris and me.

"Lemar, you need to shut your joint head ass up, and sit yo' ass down, so I can smoke yo' ass." I boldly said, so that the whole class could hear.

The whole class laughed, which embarrassed Lemar. He got up and swung at me, and I moved my head just in time, but I felt the air behind his swing.

"Damn Lemar, I sorry."

My words hurt him, and I didn't mean for that to happen.

"You play too damn much, Shanna!"

"Lemar, I said that I was sorry, you talk about me too."

Lemar was pissed off with me for a long time, but eventually we made amends.

Once school got good, it stayed good. I made a lot of friends, and I was passing my classes, well most of them. And I found some weed smokers at the school, which widened my supply source. Mrs. Landers started seeing me less because I was either at school or outside hanging out until my curfew, and when I came in, I went to my room and went to sleep.

"Shanna, you have to start cleaning up around here. Patricia do everything around here." Ms. Landers huffed one night.

"No she don't because the house ain't clean, and when am I gonna get some new clothes or something?"

"What? You is neva home, I know you over there wit' Rich laying up, get him to buy you some clothes!"

"He don't get money for me from the foster care people, you do. And I don't be ova his house all the time."

I was never over Rich's any more despite his calls and stopping by. We were finished.

"When you come in you high, and you smell like liquor."

"I don't come in here high, I'm jus' tired."

"What chu tired fo'? You don't work, Patricia work and go to school."

I was so tired of Mrs. Landers comparing me with Patricia that I wanted to scream, but I just kept my feelings to myself. I thought if I stayed in and cleaned and went to church that I would be able to get a new wardrobe or something for doing the right things. So that's what I did for a couple of weeks, but she still didn't give me money for clothes.

While I was cleaning the house, I came across a baby photo of Patricia, and on the back of it was another name, as a matter of fact, her first and last names were different. I took the picture to Mrs. Landers, and she immediately snatched the picture out of my hand.

Patricia wasn't Mrs. Lander's birth child. Mrs. Landers became more strict and bitchy towards me after I saw the photo, but I had to deal with it because I didn't want to move right away. I kept doing my chores around the house, and I went to that store front Ms. Landers called her church. And finally, she started giving me allowance, and it was five dollars more than I expected.

The winter was coming, so I got a new coat. It was a black fashion coat, and I bought some Cabbage Patch doll house-shoes and that was it. The rest of my clothes were from a thrift store, or someone gave Mrs. Landers clothes to give to me. I was too happy about my new coat and house-shoes.

I went to school in my new coat, and this older girl I used to hang out with in the girl's bathroom had commented on the coat.

"Girl, what you doing wit' a coat like this? You should let me wear it." The potential supermodel said.

It felt good to get a complement from this girl because all of the girls wanted to be just like her. She wore a lot of makeup, and she looked like a model.

"I don't think I should let you wear my coat, but thanks."

"Foreal girl, you let me wear your coat, and I'll let you wear mines."

Then she went in her locker and got her coat that was a quilted coat, but mine looked better, but for some dumb reason, I let this girl talk me into letting her wear my coat. I guess I was trying to get close to the girl, and I thought I should trust her. The next day the girl didn't come to school, and I started to become worried. For weeks I didn't see the girl or my coat, and no one else seemed to have seen her either.

One day I saw her in the hall, and I chased her down and asked her for my coat. I never knew her name only knew her face. That made me look extra stupid.

"I got your coat, girl! It's at home."

Of course I never saw my new coat again.

Eventually, Mrs. Landers asked me about the coat, and I told her what happened and she said that I'll never get anything from her again.

I started cutting classes, especially the ones I didn't like and got high with anyone who had weed. I always went to algebra because my hommies were in there, and they appreciated my sense of humor. I was getting popular with the get high crowd, and even got a nickname, "Crazy Shanna," and I thought that was cool. I was getting behind in my classes, and I really thought I would be able to catch up, but high school was different. We were learning new stuff in the classes, so I was really behind. One day I was smoking a joint in the girl's locker room, and this girl approached me.

"Let me get some of that."

"You sure you want to take a hit of this?"

"Yeah, I'm sure."

So I let the girl take a couple of pulls off of the joint, and the girl snapped. She started to laugh uncontrollably and put us at risk for getting busted.

"Girl, keep quite you gonna get us busted."

"Fuck you!"

"What?"

"Fuck you!" She insisted.

I left her ass in the locker room by herself and made my way outside. The next day, this bully named Tammie confronted me.

"My girl told me you gave her some shit that made her started acting crazy, and you left huh! I should fuck you up, I never did like yo' crazy ass."

Tammie was talking from across the room. I never said anything to Tammie because I didn't like bullies.

"Shanna, what you gonna do?" Otis shouted, instigating.

I looked away and said nothing, but I was steaming on the inside.

"Shashanna, will you solve this equation on the board?" The algebra teacher called me to the board.

As I walked up to the chalkboard, Tammie yelled, "I don't know why yo' ass is going up to the board, yo' ass can't solve shit."

After I solved the equation and got the teacher's approval. I laid the chalk down while Tammie was still talking shit. Instead of me going back to my seat, I went towards Tammie.

"Awh shit, here she come, Tammie!" Otis said while putting his hand over his mouth.

Before Tammie could get out of her seat, I struck her across her head with my fist, repeatedly.

I had my first fight in high school, and I got my first detention with the Assistant Principal, but Tammie never bothered me again.

The Assistant Principal, Dr. Brazil, was one of the most influential people in my life. He looked like Jessie Jackson, except he was bald at the top of his head with long hair on the sides. He said that I was getting into too much trouble, and I needed to be close to him, or I was going to be suspended or kicked out.

I had to go to Dr. Brazil's office every day during study period to file papers or whatever he wanted me to do, as long I was doing something constructive. Everybody liked Dr. Brazil, and students were in and out of his office all the time. There was a girl who was in his office, as I was, which made me curious about her.

She must have been curious about me too because after our second day of eying each other she asked, "Didn't you fight that girl Tammie a couple of days ago?"

"Yeah, why you want to know?"

"I was just asking. What's yo' name?"

The mean looking but pretty girl acted as if she wanted my autograph.

"Shanna."

"I see you in the halls, but I didn't know where you was coming from."

"Where I'm coming from?" I asked.

"Are you cool or not, I hate these phony ass girls in this school."

I instantly liked her.

"What's yo' name?" I asked.

"Kim."

"I see you all the time too, but like you I didn't say nothin'." I confessed.

Kim introduced me to her two friends, Tangy and Senique, who were cool as hell too. After talking for a few days, we were inseparable, and when you saw one you saw all three of us.

Finally, I fit in with a crowd at my high school. Kim, Tangy, and Senique smoked more weed than I did. I really liked them. My grades were already slipping, even Algebra, but once I got with a crowd, the party was on at school. I cut more classes than I went to, and I stayed high.

My first high school grades were all F's, and Mrs. Landers started getting calls from school about my class absences. I was getting deeper into trouble. Even the school police officer knew my name.

No one ever cared about my grades in school but me; I was never confronted nor was I punished. I was just a foster kid who was expected to do the wrong things and act out. Dr. Brazil was the only adult who seemed to care, but it wasn't enough, at least at the time.

Mrs. Landers was getting fed up with me and I knew it, but I didn't care. Hanging out with my girls was all I wanted to do because we smoked weed and drank forties. One day I came into the house so drunk that I couldn't hold my head up, and I threw up in the kitchen sink. Mrs. Landers was pissed off. I woke up Sunday morning with a hang over, but I was forced to go to church, so I was in church with a hangover, smelling like alcohol. I did my best to hold myself together, but I couldn't make it to the bathroom, and I threw up during the service, and everybody knew it.

"Shanna, you okay?" One of the church kids asked.

"Yeah, my stomach hurt!"

"I know why. You smell like you had drunk too much."

"Whateva." I replied.

Mrs. Landers was very disappointed, but why should I care about her feelings because she definitely didn't care about mine.

Back at school, the clique me, Kim, Tangy ,and Senique had was fading. It seemed like every time I attempted to make a connection with friends I was forced to detach and move on.

"You know Senique is pregnant!" Kim said in disappointment.

"When you hear this?" I asked.

"I went ova to huh house to see why she wasn't coming to school, and she told me!"

"Damn, she was the quiet one!" I said.

"The quiet ones is the ones who are sneaky." Kim said with her arms folded.

"Senique go to school for pregnant girls now, and we ain't gonna see huh nomo'!" Kim announced.

"Damn, that's a damn shame!" Tangy said while rolling her eyes.

"Tangy, if you ain't careful, it can happen to you." Kim said.

"Kim, I'm careful, baby. My momma ain't raise no fool!"

I was hurt because my girls at school were going their separate ways, and I knew my time at Ms. Landers home was coming to an end. Things came to head on a Sunday morning before church. I was hung-over and feeling mean.

Someone told Rich's mother that I came over to her house a couple of times while she was at work, and she told Ms. Landers.

"You did it this time. Momma is tired of your shit, and you gonna have to go."

Patricia's right eye floated when she was angry.

"First of all, that ain't yo' momma, and second, she can speak fo' huhself."

"That is my momma, what chu talking 'bout, bitch?"

I looked at Patricia and then I looked at Mrs. Landers, and she gave me a look that said I better not mention the adoption, so I didn't.

Mrs. Landers finally had something to say, but it wasn't nice, and then I knew my time was up.

"Eleanor told me you and Rich be fuckin' in huh house while she at work. You was supposed to be in school! Rich, wit' his grown ass, should be ashamed of hisself. He knows you a foster girl, and he can go to jail fuckin' wit' you. I should call the police on the both of y'all and have them to take you ass out of my house. You midas well pack yo' shit, cuz I called yo' worker, and she is coming to get you tomorrow. Naw, I want you out of my house right naw!"

I couldn't get a word in. I felt a little sad, but I was ready to leave Mrs. Landers house because I was treated like a foster child, and she was money hungry.

I packed my small amount of clothes into another garbage bag then sat on the couch waiting for the worker to arrive. I didn't know that social workers worked on Sundays.

When the worker got there, Ms. Landers said, "Take care Shanna and come back to visit me to go to church sometimes."

That was the last time I saw Ms. Landers.

CHAPTER 17

It Keeps Getting Better (A Vicious Cycle)

I arrived at the emergency placement after dark. It was a home, but I don't remember the people; I remember the conversation being like others.

"This is the young lady that I was telling you about. She's only staying until tomorrow, and thank you for letting her stay at your home."

"No problem."

"Shashanna, I will have to do some paper work tonight, and we'll find you a more permanent home tomorrow, ok?" The stressed out worker would say. "Okay?"

I would nod nonchalantly. Eight placements in two years, all I knew was being an outsider. The only constant I had in my life was going to school.

The next morning I woke up thinking about Carl and Momma. I missed them both and wondered if they missed me. That was how I thought about them - in passing . . . because my life was all jumbled up.

I had slept in my street clothes and used my plastic bag of stuff for a pillow instead of the pillow on the bed.

The worker picked me up as promised. The home she took me to wasn't much to look at on the outside, but the inside was very nice.

The first thing I noticed was the picture window. I adored picture windows because the vast view made me feel free. But the feeling of freedom left as soon as the lady of the house opened her mouth.

"Come on in, but take yo' shoes off."

The lady was as light as me and had medium length hair. We took our shoes off and sat in the front room. There was wall-to-wall blue carpet, white furniture, chandeliers, and sheer blue curtains. I sat in awe until the worker and the lady finished the paper work.

"Shashanna," the worker called me.

"Huh."

"This is Mrs. Jakes. Mrs. Jakes, this is Shashanna." The social worker introduced us.

Mrs. Jakes' face didn't have an expression I could read; looking at her was like looking at a lamp. There was no emotion there.

In a low voice, I heard the worker saying, "Be good, Shashanna."

When the worker left Mrs. Jakes immediately gave me my shoes, and a tall man appeared behind her.

"This is my husband, Mr. Jakes."

"What's your name, young lady?" The tall man asked.

"How you say yo' name?" Mrs. Jakes interrupted.

"Sha..shan..na!" I had enunciated.

"Stan, take 'Sha sha na' bags to her room. You can get up and go to the kitchen with me, Sha shan na."

"You hungry?" Mrs. Jakes asked in monotone.

"No." I replied.

We walked through a small kitchen while Mr. Jakes carried my clothes down some stairs.

"Come on, let me show you around the house. It's not big, but it's mine."

I followed Mrs. Jakes around the house and listened to her brag on every room in the house.

"You like this house?"

"Yeah."

I was impressed. It was the prettiest house I had ever seen.

"You heard of Muhammad Ali?"

"Yeah."

"This use to be his house when he stayed in Chicago."

"Foreal."

After the grand tour, Mrs. Jakes walked me down to the dungeon like basement that had a totally different feel. There were brown wood panels on the wall and a big tiled area.

"This is yo' room," Mrs. Jakes had positioned her arm like an usher.

I opened the door and saw three girls in the room. I thought that it was weird that I didn't hear or see them until I opened the bedroom door. The girls looked at me and waved hello, and I waved back. One in particular spoke to me.

"My name is Veronica, what's yours?"

"Shashanna!"

"That's a pretty name, I like it!"

"Thanks."

Veronica was a tall, skinny, dark chocolate girl with a sunny disposition. I noticed that there was no TV in the room and no windows. I went to bed where Mr. Jakes put my plastic bag. Mrs. Jakes went back up the stairs.

Veronica asked, "What grade you in?"

"I'm a freshman."

"I'm in eighth grade, next year I will be in high school like you."

The other two weren't talking, so I wasn't talking to them. I knew how to be the new girl. I needed to use the bathroom, so I walked towards the stairs.

"Where you going?" One of the two quite ones asked.

"To the bathroom," I said with attitude. "Not that it is any of your business."

"You can't use da bafroom upstairs because we have our own bafroom down here."

"Where?"

"In the back, we have to use that one. And we can't go upstairs unless Mrs. Jakes calls us up there."

She was chubby and light, like Mrs. Jakes; she could have been her natural daughter.

"First of all, what's yo' name, and second, can you say anything other than telling me what I can't do?" I asked.

"I'm Sonya, and I can say plenty, I jus' don't like you."

"So, I don't like you either," I said.

I knew how to get people off my back.

I left the room looking through the dungeon basement for the bathroom. Inside the small bathroom was a claw tub, a hanging shower and a tiny toilette. I closed the heavy door, and unexpectedly started crying. My life was changing again, and again, I was living with strangers, and again, I had to prove myself at a home. Home was the place where there should be peace. I had no peace in my life. I had no home, only placements. I was tired, so very tired, so I cried.

Someone knocked on the door, "It's me Veronica. Are you ok?"

I wasn't, but I didn't know her.

"I'm ok. I will be out in a minute."

I washed my hands and wiped my tears and my feelings away. I looked in the tiny round mirror of the face bowl and lifted my head high.

When I stepped out of the bathroom, there was another girl waiting to go in.

"What's up, I'm Trooty."

She looked like dude, or a want-to-be-dude.

"Hi." I said as I kept walking.

"Ain't you gonna tell me yo' name?"

I wanted to say no, but I told her, "Shanna."

"What you got a attitude or something?" Trooty said in baritone.

I walked to my room not answering her. Trooty followed me.

"I was talking to you."

I was thinking not this shit again, not another she/he thinking they were tough. Trooty scared me, but I had been scared before, and I had defended myself before. It was all too familiar.

Trooty didn't follow me into the room as I expected, so I relaxed a bit and stretched on the bed and tried to take a nap. I must have fallen asleep because we were all called upstairs to the kitchen to eat dinner, but I didn't go. I wasn't hungry, and I didn't want to go. The bed was ok with me.

I rolled over and saw Trooty standing in the bedroom doorway, "You don't want our food; you think you too good or something?"

I didn't answer.

She slammed the bedroom door closed.

I laid on the bed not sleeping and trying not to think because I didn't want to start crying again. I closed my eyes and wished hard that my life was different. I must have fallen off to sleep again because the three coming back in the room woke me up. I was thirsty, so I stood up and walked towards the stairs.

"Mrs. Jakes don't like us to go upstairs without permission, I already told you that," came from Sonya.

I ignored her and went up the stairs. Once I got in the kitchen, I cut on the lights; I didn't want anyone to think I was sneaking around. What I saw shocked me; Mrs. Jakes had a lock on her refrigerator door. I had never seen anything like that in my entire life. I took a glass out of the rack and filled it with tap water and went back downstairs.

"You can't drink or bring dishes down here. I'm telling Trooty!" Sonya spoke again.

"Damn, what the fuck can y'all do here, and I don't care who you tell. It's just water, damn." I was tired of her and frustrated.

"Yeah, I'm tired of this shit too; the new girl is right."

I looked to see who was talking; it was the other quite girl.

"We can't do shit around here, and that shit is getting old."

"What's yo' name?" I asked

"Josie."

She smiled at me, and I smiled back.

"We had a good dinner, Shanna. Catfish and corn, you missed it." Veronica said.

Her bed was next to mine, and Sonya and Josie were across the room.

"Dang, I like catfish, but I wasn't hungry."

"It was good."

The three were putting on the nightgowns.

"And I am tired of going to bed at nine o'clock. We need some changes around here." Josie said to Sonya.

"Shh, Trooty goona hear you."

"Good."

Veronica went to the light switch and flicked the lights off.

"Good night everybody," she said in her fairytale voice.

"Good night Veronica," I said because no one else answered her.

My first night at Ms. Jakes' house was horrible, and I couldn't sleep. I felt like someone, Trooty or Sonya, might try something.

In the morning, Veronica woke me up with, "It's your turn in the shower. We finished, and breakfast is in a little while."

She had such a sweet voice that I didn't get mad at her for waking me. Everybody was up and dressing but me. I hurried through my shower and got dressed.

At the breakfast table, Mrs. Jakes asked, "Shashanna, you settling in good?" while blowing the steam off her coffee.

"Mmm," was my reply.

I was sitting between Veronica and Trooty, and on the other side of the small table were Sonya and Josie. Mrs. Jakes was at the head.

Before I could finish my answer, Tooty blurted out, "Mrs. Jakes, these girls don't like being here, and they don't have to be here if they don't want to, do they?"

Mrs. Jakes ignored Trooty.

"Is everything all right, Shanna?'

"I am just getting use to the rules, and I didn't know Trooty was in charge, that's all."

Trooty stood up, "You need to shut up, new girl. You don't know what's up around here."

Mrs. Jakes put her coffee mug down.

"Is Trooty messing with y'all?"

Everybody but me shook their heads from left to right to gesture no.

"So it's just you, Shanna?"

"Naw, she ain't messing with me. I just didn't know she was in charge."

I looked down at my cereal and ate. I had spoken my piece.

"The only people in charge of anything in this house is me and my husband, Shanna. Understand?"

"Yes, ma'am."

I was told many times before that I had an old soul, which means that I was ahead of my time, and I knew bullshit when I heard it, and that house was full of it.

"Trooty, I would like to see you upstairs."

Mrs. Jakes stood and left the table. I did not care about the others not speaking up; I was getting Trooty off of my back.

Sonya quickly turned to me and whispered, "You got to be careful now."

Getting a warning from her surprised me. Trooty came back in the kitchen and joined us for breakfast.

"Shanna," Mrs. Jakes called me upstairs to her room.

I followed the blue carpet up the stairs.

The room, bed, the dresser, and tables were huge. I had never seen a master bedroom, which is what Mrs. Jakes called the room.

"Mrs. Jakes?" I said.

"Hey Shashanna, come on in here and sit down."

I sat on her bed because the chairs had stuff in them. She opened her closet and pulled out her fur coats and told me I could feel them. I did. Then she went into her dresser drawer and pulled out this pouch and unzipped it; there were stacks of hundred dollar bills. I wanted to ask for one.

"You like all of this?"

"Yeah," I answered, still trying to figure out how to ask for a hundred dollar bill. Next, she showed me at least three pistols. "Can I hold one?"

"Naw, you too young. I use these for protection because I have property; a building and a car wash."

"You must be rich?"

"No, just comfortable."

The lady had a lot of stuff. I knew my allowance was going be more than fifteen or twenty dollars a month. I wondered why Mrs. Jakes was showing me these things.

"You can have this life too, Shanna. I see it in you. Understand?"

I didn't. I had no idea why she showed me all that stuff. I left her room confused and without a hundred dollar bill. Trooty approached me on the basement steps.

"What did she say to you?"

"Nothing," I tried to get past Trooty quickly.

"Why she call you to huh room then?"

"I don't know, ask huh."

"I see that I'm gonna have to fuck you up, I don't like yo' ass." Trooty cracked her knuckles.

"You not gonna 'fuck me up', and will you move out my way?"

Trooty moved, and as I passed, she kicked at me, but I blocked it and went down the stairs. Trooty came behind me, and I had no choice but to hit her with what was closest, a ceramic soap tray.

I bloodied her face, but she kept coming. She hit me so hard that I fell to the floor. Veronica started crying, Josie ran upstairs and got Mrs. Jakes, who eventually pulled Trooty off of me.

When I got up, I saw an open gash in Trooty's head. I couldn't believe that I did that much damage. Mrs. Jakes had to take her to the doctor. Veronica, Sonya, and Josie looked at me as if I was a hero for fighting the house bully. My jaw was sore, but nothing was bleeding. I blocked most of her blows.

"She gonna talk shit, but she ain't gonna mess with you no more," Josie said.

I hoped she was right.

The social worker came to see me that evening. Mrs. Jakes didn't mention the fight, and I didn't either. The worker came to tell me that I could keep going the same high school, and she brought me a bus pass and lunch card. That was the best news I had received in a couple of days.

CHAPTER 18

I Don't Care

When I got back to school, everything was different. Since I failed math, my buddies were gone. I had the class with a bunch of strangers, and that was how it was in every class, and all girls in my clique had transferred or gotten kicked out. It was just me again, like I was at a new school, at least in the classes. But, my reputation helped me to find new people to get high with, so it wasn't like being totally new.

But, I had another problem with school; my gums were swelling and bleeding. At first, I thought I was brushing my teeth too hard, but then I would wake up with blood on my pillow. I thought I had gingivitis or something. Anyway, the kids at school noticed, and they made my life hell. They called me pregnant gums because my gums were swollen between my teeth, so I naturally I responded by teasing them, which got me into more fights. I was failing my classes again, fighting, and getting high at school. Once I started back to getting high at school, I started back to getting high after school.

I had no balance: it was party, party, and more party. I met friends whose parents worked, and that pretty much ended my attending school for a while. I left Mrs. Jakes house like I was going to school, and most days I went up until division where they took attendance, but after that I was gone.

I was back in the old neighborhood, and for my partying, things couldn't have been better. One of the first people I hooked up with was Pam.

I had just escaped from school and was darting down a side street when I heard, "Girl, where you been? Tony the weed man been asking about you."

Pam ran straight into my hug. We laughed and caught up with each other right there in the middle of the street. We decided to go over to Tony's house and see what was up with him.

He had a lot of people over to his house, so we joined the party. The more I got high, the better I felt, and I would temporaly forget about school and everything else.

The guy sitting next to me at Tony's was smoking cigarettes, and I hated the smell of cigarette smoke.

"Can you sit somewhere else with that, I'm coughing." I protested.

"If cigarettes bother you so much, why don't you move?" The guy suggested.

"I was here first." I said.

"I guess you have to smell the smoke then. You want one, it'll boost yo' high."

"No thank you."

"Here take a pull, just one, and if you don't like it, I won't bother you nomo'." The guy handed me the stinky cigarette. "Just one pull."

I caved in and inhaled the Benson and Hedges cigarette and coughed, but the cigarette did make me dizzy and confused; it was getting me higher.

"Give me one of yo' cigarettes."

"I told you," the guy smiled and handed me a cigarette.

After Tony kicked everybody out, I didn't want to go back to Mrs. Jakes' house right away. Pam and I ran into Rich's sister, Renee, on the street.

"Where you been, girl? I haven't seen you in a long time."

"I moved ova East."

"I'm about to go out wit' some friends, y'all wanna come?"

Pam answered, "No, I got to get in before my moms," and she ran off.

"We going to this lounge to have a few drinks then we going to tha lake, you think you can kick it?"

I was already high from smoking and drinking, so my sixteen year old self had only one answer, "Yeah, I can kick it."

"Don't worry about getting in the lounge, the owner is cool wit' me." Renee bragged.

That was my first time going to a lounge, and I remember feeling kind of special.

We walked into the bar easily enough, but once we sat at the table with her friends one of them asked, "Renee, how old is yo' friend?"

"She can tell you huhself." Renee said.

"I'm sixteen." I said

"Renee, she is too young to be in here."

"She's cool, don't worry about it."

So, I sat with them and hung out, but the bartender wouldn't serve me a drink, so this older guy helped me order my drinks and paid for them. I drank so much that I started to feel dizzy, and the next thing I knew I was in the backseat of a car hearing people calling my name.

"Shanna, Shanna, wake up! Where you live so we can drop you off?"

I must have given Renee and her friends my address because I woke up at home. As soon as Renee and her friends helped me to the front door, they left.

Mr. Jakes came to the door and let me in, and I went straight to my room and fell out. I woke up the next morning with a headache that made me wish that I never went with Renee, and I swore that I would never drink again.

All of a sudden I heard, "Shanna, Shanna, breakfast is ready. Are you ok?" It was Veronica, and she was bent over me stroking my forehead. "You don't look good."

She helped me stand, and she helped me walk to the bathroom.

"I will be ok, thank you."

When I got to the kitchen with the other girls, they looked at me as if I was a wild animal.

"You got fucked up, huh?"

"Trooty, not today," I said with my head on the kitchen table.

"Shashanna, when you get finished eating, I have to talk to you." Mrs. Jakes said, standing in the doorway.

I had to go to the bathroom first before I talked to anybody. I ran down stairs and barely made to the tiny toilette; I threw up twice. I tried to steady myself, and I doused cold water on my face to bring me back.

"Fuck drinking." I said into the mirror and then I went back upstairs.

I was not in the seat good before Mrs. Jakes said, "You been getting out of hand, and I'm not gonna put up with you coming in my house drunk. You are stirring up things around here, and the girls are getting mad cuz you come in later than they do. I had this house in order before you came here."

I exhaled, "You keeping kids locked in the basement with no television is order? You think locking a refrigerator is order? You think letting Trooty bully people is order? Please." I said while holding my head from the hangover.

Mrs. Jakes face was twisted tight with anger, "Trooty has been here since she was little, and I have had girls come and go, but Trooty is like my own. Tomorrow when the agency opens, I'm gonna talk to Mrs. Roberts and see what she can do with you because she doesn't play."

I didn't know who Ms. Roberts was, and I didn't care. My head was pounding, and Mrs. Jakes words were adding to my headache.

"Can I get my allowance?"

"Naw, I'll talk to you later."

I went downstairs and Sonya and Josie were staring at me.

"Y'all got a eye problem?"

They looked away. I went in the bathroom and threw up some more. When I got back to the room, Veronica handed me a can of ginger ale.

"Drink this, it will help."

I didn't know how she knew about ginger ale and a hangover, but it did help. I was able to lay down and sleep.

The next morning, Mrs. Jakes woke me up herself.

"We got an appointment with Mrs. Roberts, be ready in twenty minutes, and please get the alcohol smell off of you. You stink."

I hadn't been to a special agency meeting sense they set up the visits with my momma. Sometimes, I forgot there was an agency. My workers changed so much that I didn't bother to keep their phone numbers. When I changed into my clean clothes, I found a joint in my dirty pants packet. I really wanted to smoke it, but I didn't.

I sat in the office chair watching thirty minutes click off the clock before they called me into the office.

The lady, Mrs. Roberts, was sitting behind a desk, and Mrs. Jakes was in a chair in front of the desk, and there was another lady sitting on a sofa off to the side, and there was an empty chair in front of the desk for me.

"Shashanna, I heard a lot of things about you." Mrs. Roberts offered me the empty chair.

I sat down rolling my eyes. I decided I didn't like her.

"Oh yeah, what you heard about me?"

"A lot, but let's talk about what's going on right now. Mrs. Jakes tells me she is having problems with you, and that you are getting out of hand, what do you think I should do?"

"I don't care because nobody care about me. Mrs. Jakes didn't care when one of her girls jumped on me."

"What? Mrs. Jakes, when did this happen?"

I knew enough about how the agency worked to get Mrs. Jakes in trouble. She never told the agency that Trooty jumped on me.

"Shanna busted the other girl's head open. I thought the matter was best handled at my home. The girls get along fine now."

"Hmph," I said, rolling my eyes.

"Mrs. Jakes, you are supposed to report all fights that happen in the home. Shashanna, do you feel safe in the home?" Mrs. Roberts rocked back in her chair.

"Most of the time."

I had to bite the inside of my cheek to keep from smiling; I finally had some leverage with Mrs. Jakes; someone was on my side.

"Ok, good. But, there are other problems at the home; mainly your staying out and drinking and possible drug use. And your disrespectful tone towards Mrs. Jakes." I began to think that maybe she wasn't on my side. "Mrs. Jakes tells me that these problems are happening more and more, and that you came home last night so drunk that Mr. Jakes had to help you downstairs."

That could have happened, I didn't remember.

Ms. Roberts was tapping her finger on the desk. Mrs. Jakes sat back in the chair, nodding her head yes. I couldn't say anything because it was all true.

"Do you hear me, young lady?"

I shook my head yes.

"Do you have anything to say, an explanation for such behavior?" I hunched my shoulders. "Ok, based on similar complaints from your other placements . . . I think it is in your best interest and the foster family's to get you some outside help." She gestured toward the lady on the sofa, "This is Mrs. Newport; she will be taking you to be evaluated by a psychiatrist."

"A psychiatrist?" I stood up.

"Yes, we have tried to put you in homes that would accommodate you, but we are running out of homes to place you in because of your behavior. So, at this point, you need some outside help…professional help. Now sit back down."

I sat back down and listened to Ms. Roberts. I felt Mrs. Roberts liked me, and I trusted her because every once in a while she would say something nice about me after saying something I had done. It wasn't all bad news with her.

"Seeing the psychiatrist is for your benefit, Shanna. Okay, let me rephrase that, would you like to see a psychiatrist, Ms. Wilson?"

"No."

"Why not?"

"I'm not crazy."

"No one is saying you are. What we are saying is you need some help."

"Why?" I blurted out with my arms folded tight.

"Because there are thing going on with you that you don't even know; you need help with your anger, trust, and adjusting, to start. I have gone to therapy myself; believe me, it helps."

Therapy didn't sound as bad as a psychiatrist.

"Let us help you with that anger that seems to get you into trouble."

"I guess."

The lady on the sofa turned out to be my new worker, Ms. Newport. We walked into another office together.

"Hi Shashanna, I have a few questions that I would like to ask. It's been reported that you use drugs and alcohol, exactly how much do you consume in one day?"

"Since you want to know, I smoke a bag of weed, and I don't know how much I drink, but I drink a lot. Anything else?"

I hate when people do not listen to me and believe what others say about me, and that was what Ms. Newport was doing.

"When you say a bag a day, what exactly do you mean?"

"Oh, about a pound."

"A pound?"

"Yeah, a pound."

"Do you use other drugs?"

"Whateva' drugs you heard I was doing."

"Shashanna, you are being unreasonable."

"Since I have to go to the shrink, I might as well act like it."

"This report will be read by the psychiatrist, and they'll evaluate you from what they have read. You don't want that."

"I don't care what none of y'all think."

After I left the agency, I felt like getting high, and I remembered the joint I found. Mrs. Jakes dropped me off at home, and I went out back and smoked the whole joint by myself.

The day had come for my first visit to the psychiatrist, so I played the part. I ripped parts of my clothes; and I didn't comb my hair. Mrs. Jakes called me upstairs to take me to my appointment.

"Hurry up, I have to be somewhere after this," she said.

When I finally made it upstairs, Mrs. Jakes looked at me and shook her head in disgust.

"Go back downstairs and fix yourself up, I don't want to be seen with you looking like that." She said while dusting off her sleeves on her leather jacket.

"I am fixed up, let's go," I said.

"You make me sick."

I wanted to say fuck you, but the look on my face must have said it for me. We didn't say word to each other on the ride to the shrink; a term I heard on television. Mrs. Jakes didn't like me, and she knew that I didn't like her.

CHAPTER 19

Moments of Clarity

When we got to the hospital the psychiatrist gave me an evaluation test on paper before he asked me questions. I marked anything and handed it back to him. He was kind of old, bald, almost skinny, and white.

He and I were alone in a little room with a white table. He sat on one side, and I sat on the other. He was flashing cards and asked what did I see on them.

"I see joints and forties." I responded while looking around the room.

"What are joints and forties?" He asked, pulling his glasses to the tip of his nose.

"Drugs and alcohol, what chu drink and smoke?"

His eyebrows went up but he didn't answer.

He put the cards down and asked, "What's two plus two?"

"I don't know."

"Young lady, go in the waiting room, and I'll call you back in."

I stormed to the waiting room where Mrs. Jakes was sitting, knowing she didn't want to be there, but it was her job. I wondered how long I had to be there because the whole situation was cutting into my social plans.

The psychiatrist called me back in the room, and he had the clipboard with the questions I had answered.

"These scores are ridiculous. Even a six year old can score higher than this. Either you're just plain stupid, or you are acting like it. If you continue to act like you are crazy you will have to come here every week or be admitted to a psych ward. Would you like that?" The doctor asked, taking off his glasses.

"Uh uh!"

I was shocked by his strong use of words and his tone.

"I advise you to take this test over and give better answers...ok?"

"Yeah, but what I'm here fo'?" I asked.

"You were referred by DCFS for behavioral issues."

"So, if I answer the questions better will I have to come back?"

"Well, not every week, but every once in a while. Are you ok with that?"

"Whateva', as long as I don't have to come here every week."

I took the test over, and I gave the best possible answers that I could.

After reviewing my new test, he said, "I knew you couldn't be as dumb as the scores made you out to be. A visit twice a month should be enough. See the receptionist to make an appointment."

After seeing the shrink, I knew that I didn't want to come back, but I knew I was expected to. Mrs. Jakes dropped me at school, and since it was after division, I stayed for the whole day. I didn't know what they were talking about in any class.

Cutting classes at school caught up with me. I got suspended the week before the grades came out. I got all F's again. It was summer, and Mrs. Jakes, Mrs. Roberts, Ms. Newport, and the school people were all talking about summer school. I was ok with that because I knew that would get me to my old neighborhood. I had no plans of attending summer classes either. I knew a lot of kids who had dropped out, and they were ok.

CHAPTER 20

Never In My Wildest Dreams

I had one very good day that summer, and I'll never forget the day. The moment is etched in my memory forever because it was one of the greatest days of my life. The foster care agency had a festival/parade, and we all had to be there. I was ordered to go against my will. By this time, Mrs. Jakes had a couple of new girls, and we all went to the event in the agency's van. The festival was in a Hispanic neighborhood, and it reminded me of Nydia and Stan from eighth grade.

The agency was one of the festival sponsors, and there were television crews and lots of food. I had no idea who was going to be at this festival because no one told me anything; I just had to be present. All of a sudden I heard these people screaming, and Mrs. Roberts came over to me and gave me a slice of watermelon and told me to give it to Mayor Harold Washington.

"I don't want to give him the watermelon," I snipped.

"It's too late, here he is. Say something, Shashanna!" Ms. Roberts was elbowing me and forced the watermelon in my arms.

"Oh, this watermelon is for you, from our agency...here," I spoke softly.

"Thank you young lady, what's your name?" The Mayor asked with a smile on his face.

"Shashanna!"

"That's a pretty name." The Mayor replied while holding the watermelon that I gave him.

After I had given the Mayor the watermelon, he pulled out a marker and asked could he autograph my arm, and I said yes.

"Nice tan Shashanna," The Mayor said in his deep voice.

"Thank you!"

I was in utter shock that Harold Washington, Chicago's first African American Mayor remembered my name.

"Shashanna, here comes the news camera; we want you to present another watermelon to the Mayor on television." Ms. Robertson was excited.

I refused the offer because I was overwhelmed and nervous. I moved out of the spotlight and let someone else be on television with our Mayor.

That same summer my mom got in touch with me. I was in the dungeon, putting my money together for a bag of weed.

"Shanna, telephone," Mrs. Jakes yelled.

I never received calls because I never gave anyone Mrs. Jakes' number. I barely knew it.

"Ok." I walked up the basement steps and went to Mrs. Jakes bedroom door and answered the phone. "Hello."

"Hi Shashanna, this is yo' mother." I didn't say anything because I was upset with my mother because of the fight we had the last time I saw her. "Are you gonna say something to me?"

"Hi," was all I could manage.

"I moved from the place I stayed at, and I want you to come and visit me."

"Why you want to see me now, all we gonna do is fight again."

"Shashanna, that should have never happened. I don't want to talk about that. I want to see you because I miss you, okay?"

So many negative thoughts went through my head, and I couldn't find one decent word to say to my mother.

"Ok, whateva'," I responded.

"Shanna," When my mother said my name she dragged it, Shaaaaana, and I hated it. "I didn't like what you did, Shanna, you got drunk, and you only a child."

"And don't forget I had sex wit' yo' man too." I said with attitude.

"We don't stay together anymo'. I live somewhere else, and I want you to come over."

"Why you want me to come over?" My mother started to cry; she always cried, so I caved in. "Okay, when you want me to come over, and wut's yo' address?"

I got a piece of paper and a pen from the kitchen and wrote my mother's information down.

"I love you Shanna." I never believed my mother when she said she loved me. That was just how I felt. "Can I call you at this number again?" She asked.

"You have to ask Mrs. Jakes."

I gave the phone to Mrs. Jakes. My mother and Mrs. Jakes started talking, and I went downstairs and thought about my mother. Deep inside I wanted to see her again.

I wondered was she still doing drugs, and was she at a better place than the last. I put the piece of paper with mother's phone number and address under my mattress.

That same night, Mrs. Jakes had a party at her house, and it was crowed; people filled up the backyard. The night before, Trooty left and didn't come home, and a new girl moved in. We were told to stay in our room. I snuck out when the party got started and bought a bag weed.

I smoked a joint, so I was a little high. When I got back, Veronica was still in the room. In the kitchen was a barrel with a variety of beer and coolers, so I took two. I offered Veronica one, but she said no. The new girl was sleep or acted sleep.

"You gonna get sick," Veronica warned me.

"If I do, you will take care of me."

She smiled when I said that.

"I'ma be in high school with you next year. We gonna ride the bus together."

"Yep," I said draining the first cooler, "You gonna like it, a lot cool boys there."

"Boys make me sick."

I didn't know if Veronica was born different or had something happen to her. I knew I liked her, and that was enough for me. I went back upstairs to get another cooler, and they were all gone, so I grabbed a beer. I smelled weed and looked out the back door and saw Mr. Jakes and a couple of his friends getting high.

I went downstairs and told Veronica.

"Yeah, he smoke it all the time at night."

"Fo' real?"

"Yeah, all the time."

"You get high?"

"No! It is bad for you." I still liked her. "You like to, don't you?" She asked.

"How you know?"

"You smell like it all the time."

I laughed and hugged her. Veronica was really looking forward to going to high school with me, and that made me think about going back and really trying, but I didn't want to be a freshman again. My pride wouldn't let me think about taking classes with Veronica.

Before school started, Ms. Roberts called me and told me Mrs. Jakes wanted me out of her house because I was still staying out late and coming home drunk. She told her I was smoking weed in her house and drinking.

I didn't care, but I was going to miss Veronica. She cried when I left. No one had ever cried about me leaving, so I cried with her.

CHAPTER 21

Too Good To Be True

"Ms. Newport, where am I'm going this time?"
"You are going to be moving near the agency."
That was really cool because the agency wasn't too far from the school's neighborhood.
"Shashanna, I hope you do well in this home because we can't seem to find people who will put up your behavior. Ms. Harris is new to the agency, and you will be one of her first kids."
On our way to my new home, Ms. Newton gave me a pep talk and told me I was running out of placement options.
"Shanna, please try to stay here more than six months."
I sat looking out of the window of the car because I didn't care.
"Send me to my momma."
"She's not stable Shanna, so she is not an option."

I hadn't talked to my mother since the phone call, and I told myself I didn't care.

When we arrived at the home there were people on the porch, and the block was busy. I felt good about the home already.

"Is Valerie Harris here?" Ms. Newton asked the people on the porch.

"Yes, that's my momma, let me go get huh."

A rotund lady came to the door.

"Hi, is this my girl?" The lady asked with a hearty greeting.

"Yes, her name is Shashanna. Can we come in?"

"Yes, yes, where is my manners?"

The house wasn't rich looking like Mrs. Jakes, but it had a homely feel to it and from the start, I knew that I would like living there.

"I'm Ms. Harris, how are you, Shashanna?"

"I'm fine." I was smiling.

Ms. Harris was a lady with extra big breasts that pointed straight out because of her Playtex bra. She had a Jheri curl, and a fat lady odor.

"You can put your stuff by the door, and my son Tom will take them to yo' room. You will be sharing a room with one other girl, and huh name is Lequisha." Ms. Harris yelled, "Tom!"

I heard a distant voice that answered, "What?"

"This is the new girl, Shash…"

"Sha-shan-na!" I finished my name for Ms. Harris.

"Shashanna," she got it right.

"Hey!" Tom greeted.

Tom was this short kid who I knew was trouble because he seemed spoiled like weed.

"Hi!" The other girl, Lequisha, came down to see me too.

Lequisha looked like another she/he. She had a deep voice and was dressed in men's basketball gear. She had French braids going to the back of her head.

Ms. Newport and Ms. Harris finished the paper work.

"Alright Ms. Harris, I'll be on my way! Shashanna, don't give Ms. Harris any problems, okay!"

"She alright." Ms. Harris assured her.

"I'll talk to you soon, Ms. Harris." Ms. Newport said on her way out.

I sat on the dirty chase sofa, knowing that I was placed in a home with little restrictions because of the way the house looked, and the fact that Ms. Harris was a new foster parent.

"Shanna honey, you want something to eat?"

"No, I ate right befo' I got here, maybe later."

"You ain't going to give me any trouble is you?" Ms. Harris gave me the suspicious eye.

"No, ma'am."

"Come on, let me show you to yo' room. Lequisha, get some sheets and stuff for Shanna, can I call you Shanna?"

"Yeah, everybody does."

"I think you gonna like it here. When everybody come in, you'll meet the rest of the family."

When I got to the room, Ms. Harris left me. Lequisha was sitting on her bed quietly.

"When did you get here?" I asked Lequisha.

"I been here about a month."

"Awe, okay."

Tom walked in and asked, "Why you in foster homes, your momma left you?" I gave Tom the evil eye, so he would stop harassing me with kid questions that actually hurt. "Forget you then," Tom left me alone.

"He stupid, don't pay him any attention. Let's go meet the family."

We walked back to the living room and more people came in the house.

"Who is this?" One guy asked.

"When she get here?" Another guy asked.

"This is the new girl, Shanna. Shanna, these are my nephews and grandson, Mane, and Dre."

"Hey girl, I'm gonna make sure you are comfortable here." Mane said in a flirting tone.

"Leave that girl alone, Mane. You know betta." Ms. Harris told him.

"I'm jus' being polite, Auntie…calm down."

Mane was a grown man, living with his aunt. Dre was younger than Mane, and dark and cute. He didn't speak directly to me.

It was a lot of people in the house.

"Let's go out on the porch," Lequisha said.

"Hey!" Somebody spoke.

"Hi!" I spoke back.

"Who is you?"

"Shashanna!"

"You momma's new girl or sumthin'?"

"Yeah, you can say that."

From the doorway Ms. Harris said, "Shanna, this is my daughter, Sharon."

Sharon was dark, big-boned, and had a Jheri curl like her mother, and she had bucked teeth.

I was bombarded on the porch with questions from damn near everybody, but it was cool. Somebody lit a joint, and Sharon opened a forty. They passed me both, and I accepted. It was more freedom than I had ever had at a placement. The questions stopped, and I listened to the neighborhood happenings until I got tired. When I left the porch more people had joined the crowd. Ms. Harris' house was the spot.

I went up to the room and laid in my bed.

"How you like it here so far?" Laquisha asked.

"I like it, do you?"

"Yeah, but I miss my family. I go and see them every weekend. You see your parents?" Leqiusha asked me.

"I see my mom every once in a while. You haven't been to a lot of foster homes have you, Lequisha?"

"Naw, this is my first one and hopefully my last one."

She talked more about her family, but I heard little because I thought about mine. I thought about my brother Carl, and wondered how he and his new family were doing.

While we were talking, it seemed like everybody came in and interrupted our conversation, but I liked it. I couldn't believe how this family had welcomed me into their home. For the first time at a placement, I slept the first night without an eye open.

The next day, I learned that the weed was around the corner, and Ms. Harris was cool with us drinking beer. It was too cool to be real. The bummer came when I found out if I went back to school I would have to be a freshman; there was no way around it, even if I transferred schools. School was over for me, at least for a while.

I didn't have to lie about not going because Ms. Harris worked days, and Ms. Newport was trying to find me an alternative. She mentioned GED classes, but I was loving the freedom of not going to school. I was in a place where partying was ok. So, I partied.

I made a lot of friends with the neighborhood people, and they embraced me quickly. Mane was trying to get with me every day, and I was surprised that he didn't try to come in my bedroom while I was sleep. I was getting popular in the neighborhood, and I was unsupervised most of the day.

I felt totally free, and curfew wasn't an issue as long as I was on the porch. Everybody got high in the house except for Tom and Ms. Harris. Lequisha and I had gotten close, and she taught me how to repair a broken cigarette because we didn't have money to buy cigarettes, so we begged for them. I was comfortable and stress free. I was having the time of my life.

Every six months, DCFS would evaluate me, and for the first time, I knew that I was going to get a good report, so I was looking forward to it.

Mrs. Roberts did the interview in her office.

"Ms. Harris, how is Shashanna adjusting to your home?"

"I don't have a problem with Shanna. She is a nice young lady."

"Good," Mrs. Roberts blew a sigh of relief and smiled at me.

"Shashanna, you seem to be adjusting to Ms. Harris' house well, keep up the good work. What about school?"

"Thinking about it, a lot." I lied.

"Well, you are smart young lady, and you did do well at times. So, since your home environment is better, I think you should consider buckling down with the books."

I didn't want to lie to Mrs. Roberts, so I only smiled and nodded my head. Mrs. Roberts brought us lunch because my report was so good.

That same day, when we got home, the school called me. I think Mrs. Roberts had something to with it. The counselor told me I was demoted and would have to take freshman classes, but she said with summer school and night school, I could get back on track. I thought about seeing Veronica, and I thought the people I knew that had dropped out, all they did was get high.

I thought about how much I liked school when I did what I was supposed to do. For some reason, I thought about the Mayor; he didn't drop out. Mrs. Roberts could have been right; maybe since I was happy at home, I would do better at school. I made up my mind before I got off the phone with the counselor. I would try again. I would get back on track.

I went to school the next day. I was eager to set things right. I attended every class. I visited Dr. Brazil, and he told me it was good to see me and how proud he was of me for coming back. I did good in my classes because a lot of the work was review. I looked for Veronica but didn't see her. I was going to wait a couple of days then call Mrs. Jakes' house.

It really felt good to be at school doing the right thing. The teachers remembered me, but they didn't embarrass me. A couple kids gave me a hard time at first, but I ignored them because they weren't doing anything I couldn't do if I wanted to. And, if I wanted to get high I could do it at home.

My midterm grades were all B's. I called Mrs. Roberts, and she sent me a watch.

Dr. Brazil told me, "I knew you could."

Things were good and I felt good and the school nurse told me it was the Epilepsy medicine that had my gums swollen. She gave me a note for my doctor, and I got a new prescription. Things stayed good until a week before report cards.

Ms. Harris came into our bedroom and told us, "You and Lequiesha have to move tomorrow," she said with tears in her eyes.

"Why?" We both asked simultaneously.

"I'm having problems wit' my license, and both yo' workers coming to get y'all tomorrow."

I didn't try to stop the tears. I was hurt bad, and I collapsed on the bed and cried.

"When I get my license back, I'm gonna ask could you come back here, okay Shanna honey?"

She sat on the bed and tried to comfort me, but I rolled away from her. I knew it was all too good to be real. I stopped crying and stood up.

Lequisha asked, "Damn, why they doing this?"

"Because we foster kids, and don't nobody give a fuck."

Ms. Harris promised me that she would fight to get me back into her home, but I knew better, nobody fought for me.

CHAPTER 22

Bad Behavior, Bad Decisions

Ms. Newport tried to get me talking in the car. I had been to so many foster homes that leaving was part of my life. I tried to be hard, but leaving Ms. Harris' hurt. We arrived at a house that looked like a barn, and the lady looked like she was still in the nineteen seventies.

Mrs. Newport introduced herself and me.

"Hi, I'm the person you spoke to on the phone…Mrs. Newport."

"Hi, I've been expecting you, come on in." The lady said while opening the screen door.

She was wearing a uniform.

"This is the young lady I've talked to you about. Her name is Shashanna. Shashanna, this is Ms. Seth. Say hello Shashanna."

Ms. Newport knew that I was upset, so she elbowed me.

"Hi!"

"You not gonna give me any trouble are you?" The lady said while looking over her glasses. I shook my head no. "I'll introduce you to the girls when they get home from school."

"Shashanna has been reinstated into school and doing a lot better." Ms. Newport said.

"Well, in order to stay here, you have to be in school…got it?"

"Yeah."

As soon as Mrs. Newport left, Ms. Seth lectured me about the rules of the house and what she doesn't like. I heard Ms. Seth, but I didn't listen because it was the same rules from other homes. I was tired.

"Let me show you to your room."

In the room was a set of bunk beds and a single twin bed on one side of the room. There were only three girls who lived at the house, including myself. While I was unpacking my belongings, I heard someone knocking on the back door. Ms. Seth opened the door, and minutes later this girl peaked in the room.

"Shashanna, this is my daughter, Kenyatta, she's been here for a while."

"Hi, Kenyatta."

"What color is you?"

"What?"

"You from Puerto Rico or something because you ain't black!"

"I am black."

"Yo' mamma black?"

"Yes!"

"What about yo' daddy?"

"Maybe he's not."

"You don't know yo' daddy?"

"Do you know yours?"

That question stopped her questions. I guessed she didn't know hers.

"Here come Sonya, you gonna like huh." Kenyatta exclaimed.

Sonya came in through the back door same as Kenyatta, so I knew we couldn't enter the house through the front door.

"Sonya, didn't you see the new girl? You gonna speak to huh?" Kenyatta instigated.

"Hi!" Sonya said with no interest.

I waved my hand instead of speaking because I didn't want to speak to someone who didn't want to speak to me.

I had a feeling that Sonya didn't like living at the home, her attitude reflected how I felt; she seemed just as tired as me. I slept the whole first day away and no one tried to wake me up, which was cool.

When I woke up, everybody was gone. I walked out of the room and entered the kitchen, and there was a note on the table.

"Shashanna, I will be back at eleven for lunch. There is some cereal and bacon in the refrigerator, help yourself."

After I cooked and ate, I walked through the house looking for nothing and got bored. I heard the front door open, and it was Ms. Seth.

"Hi Shashanna, did you read the note on the kitchen table? I hope you wasn't scared being here by yourself. Soon you will be going back to school."

"What school am I going to?" I asked.

"The same school you been going to." That was good news. "Shanna could you go to the store for me, it's right on the corner?"

"Ok," I was bored and wanted to feel the neighborhood.

At the store, this heavy Hispanic guy started hitting on me. He worked at the store.

I ignored him until he asked, "You high mommy?"

I hadn't since I started really trying in school, and at Mrs. Harris's house I chilled because Laquisha was hitting the books too. So, I hadn't got high in a while.

"Yeah, why?"

"I got what you need, mommy. I got the good weed right here. Take some of this."

He put a bag in my hand.

"How much you want for it?" I asked.

"For you, I jus' want yo' number."

"I don't have a number. Here, take this money."

"Don't worry mommy, after you smoke that you will be back. So what's up, you got a man or what?"

"Why?"

"Do you?" He persisted.

"No." I answered. I took a really good look at him and had to ask, "What are you mixed with?"

I asked him the stupid question everyone asks me.

"My mom is black and my dad is Puerto Rican. Why you ask me that, you mixed too, right? Whatever you is, I think you are beautiful. So you gonna get wit' me, or what?"

Leonard's stomach bulged over his jogging pants.

"I'll think about it."

"You should smile all the time because it looks good on you."

"Do you have a girl?"

"Not really, I'm getting divorced."

"How old are you?"

"Twenty-seven. How old is you?"

"I'm sixteen and shouldn't be talking to you."

"Age ain't nothing but a numbuh, if you don't tell, I won't tell. Keep the bag I gave you for later, and come smoke a joint with me in the back."

We walked around the back of the store to an enclosed yard.

"Here, fi' this up," Leonard handed me a joint and a lighter.

The weed was strong, "Man, this is some good weed."

"You can't pull on this too hard. This is some Afghan weed."

I didn't know what Afghan weed was, but I knew I was real high from a couple of hits.

"When I'm gonna see you again, doll face?" Leonard asked.

"Maybe tomorrow."

"I'ma hold you to that."

When I got back to the house, Mrs. Seth was standing at the backdoor waiting.

"What took so long?"

"I met a friend."

And I decided Leonard would be my friend.

"You look like you been smoking that reefer. I don't want to see you coming in my house high." Ms. Seth said calmly. "You starting out wrong with me, Shanna."

"Ok," I was too high to say anything else.

I had to catch three buses to get to school, and I didn't mind because I was still on mission at school. I wanted a report card with good grades.

Walking to the bus stop one morning, Leonard saw me and called me into the house behind the store. It was his mother's house, and he lived there with his brothers and her. We got high that morning, and I didn't go to school. I did for a couple of days, and once again, school lost to my partying.

I started hanging out at Leonard's house instead of going to school. One thing led to another with us, and we did it, and it was a lot like when I did with Rich, nothing much.

"You finished already?" I asked.

"Girl, I waited a long time for this. That was just round one."

There was no round two, Leonard went to sleep, so I stashed some weed in my pocket and left. But I left with more than Leonard's weed with me.

The school had called and reported my absences, so I started going back to school. As the weeks went by, I started feeling tired and sleepy all the time.

Kenyatta suspiciously asked, "You sure is sleeping a lot, you sick or pregnant?"

The question scared me, but I didn't answer because I had missed my period.

Ms. Seth had gotten fed up with me, and she said very little. I knew my time was up at her house, but my mind was on my missing period. I cut school and went to the doctor. I was seven weeks pregnant. Leonard got me pregnant with five seconds of sex.

I went from the doctor to his house.

He opened the door and asked, "What's up baby, come in. What's going on?"

I didn't want to beat around the bush because I needed help. I didn't know what to do.

"I'm pregnant!"

"Wut! So what you sayin'?"

"It's yours."

"How you know it's mine. We only did it one time." I looked at Leonard and didn't respond to his question. "So, what you gonna do?" He asked.

"I don't know," and I didn't.

I did not have a clue.

"Do you want to have a baby?"

"No." I knew that much

"Okay, come back later and we'll talk about it, but I got to go now."

Leonard rushed me away, and in my gut I knew he wasn't going to be much help.

When I got to Ms. Seth's house my clothes were packed up by the back door.

She walked by me and said, "Your worker is on the way," and that was all she said.

I sat at the kitchen table and thought about being pregnant. I thought about how I got pregnant. I got pregnant because I wasn't at school doing what I was supposed to be doing. If I wasn't getting high, I wouldn't got pregnant. To myself I said, *Damn, I'ma have to go to the pregnant girl school.*

CHAPTER 23

Just Drop Me Off Anywhere

I was taken to a temporary placement because the agency didn't have a permanent one for me. Ms. Newport was quite in the car, I guess she was disappointed, but I didn't care. I was so desperate about being pregnant that I almost told her about my situation.

The lady that I stayed with was Ms. Seth's friend, Ms. King. Mrs. Newport did not stay a minute. She dropped me off and left.

"Shanna, you know the agency is not gonna put up with you, so why is you acting like you do?"

"What do you mean?"

"Ms. Seth told me you is hard to handle, and she couldn't deal with you anymo'."

"She's too strict, Ms. King."

"That's because she is over protective of you girls."

"We'll can I stay here?"

"No Lordy, I can't deal with you, I'll be in the hospital or something."

I smiled and told Ms. King that I was going to lie down and rest. I fell straight to sleep and slept into the afternoon.

"You okay?" Ms. King woke me up.

"Yeah just tired."

"You look tired. You hungry?"

"Yes ma'am."

"Let's go to Wendy's."

Ms. King and I had one thing in common; we both loved Wendy's apple dumplings, and the treat was especially good to me.

"This is good ain't it, Shanna?"

"Yeah, I can eat another one."

"Me too."

And she brought us another one. When we got back, Ms. Newport was parked in front of her house.

"I talked your teachers and your counselor at the high school this morning. They were all surprised by your recent absences. They all had good reports except for your attendance. You were doing so well that you are still passing your classes. They all agreed to give you make up work."

She made me smile with that news. I still had a chance to get decent grades.

"I'm not failing?"

"No, and they want you to come back."

"Cool, I'll start going back right away."

The house she took me to was nice looking, but the foster mother was plain spooky. I didn't want to stay, but Ms. Newport wasn't hearing it. The lady showed me to a room the reeked of Pine Sol. She didn't offer me dinner or anything and didn't tell me one rule. She just left me in the room. I found some weed in my pants pocket and flushed it down the toilet. I really felt like getting high was my problem.

If I would have just kept going to school, I wouldn't have been pregnant. The teachers were willing to work with me, so I was going to work harder than ever to stay on track.

I was getting hungry, so I left my room looking for the kitchen and the spooky lady. I heard an argument, but I figured the lady was arguing with whoever else was in the house.

I found the lady standing in the kitchen arguing with herself; she was having a full-fledged argument with just her. I backed out of the kitchen and went back to my room.

The lady called me to dinner; it was pork and beans and hot dogs with a glass of Kool-Aid. While we were eating she started talking, but not to me.

"I told you last week Paul that we wear getting a new girl."

"Who are you talking to?" I asked.

"Nobody, I'm jus' trying to figure out what I'm gonna fix for desert."

"Oh, okay. I need to call Ms. Roberts about my buss pass." I lied.

"You can call her after desert."

I stopped eating, "No, I need to call her now before she gets off."

"Okay, the phone is by the icebox."

Mrs. Roberts answered on the first ring, before I could say anything the lady screamed, "What the fuck you standing there for, you scared me!"

I told Mrs. Roberts, "Y'all got to come get me; she is crazy."

I ran outside and waited on the curb.

When Ms. Newport pulled up, she went inside and got my stuff because I wasn't going back into the house. She asked me what happened, and after I told her, she started laughing. I didn't think nothing funny happened, but she did. She laughed all the back to Mrs. King's house. Mrs. King and me had Geno's pizza that night for dinner. I wanted to tell Mrs. King I was pregnant because I thought she could help, but I didn't.

The next placement was with a couple; they had a biological son and two foster boys who were mentally challenged. The foster mother had a beauty shop in her basement, and her husband used to cook beans every day, and the smell made me nauseous.

I stayed in my room because I got there on a weekend, and I had figured out that I would talk to somebody at school about being pregnant. I would say I had a friend who was pregnant and get the information. I did not want to have a baby, so I was going to ask about abortions. Just thinking about it scared me. The word sounded mean.

That Sunday night I was hungry, so I went down to the kitchen to fix me a bowl of beans because there was nothing else to eat. The man of the house was in the kitchen.

"Why you stay in the room all the time, don't you like it here?"

I just shrugged my shoulders and said, "I don't know."

I sat at the table and ate my beans.

"Can I ask you another question?"

"Yeah," I mumbled.

"Why is yo' tiddys so big?"

"Huh, what? I don't know."

I got up and left my bowl of beans.

"But, I was just giving you a compliment," he said to my back.

I stopped turned around and told him, "Don't compliment me nomo'."

"Fine, I won't talk to you any mo' then."

And he didn't.

CHAPTER 24

Déjà vu (Somebody Cares)

Instead of going to school that Monday like I planned, Ms. Newport came to get me and took me to the agency to see Mrs. Roberts. I thought they found out I was pregnant.

I was sitting in front of Mrs. Roberts' desk.

"Shanna, I wanted to personally apologize for Mrs. Jacobs."

"Who?"

"The placement you had last week; the lady that talked to herself."

"Oh, ok."

"And, I think I have some news that will make you happy."

Ms. Harris came into the office and hugged me tight, "I asked Ms. Roberts can you come and live with me again, would you like that Shanna honey?"

"Yeah, when?"

"Right now, the paper work is done. We just wanted to see how you felt about it." Mrs. Roberts said.

Mrs. Roberts and Ms. Harris made me feel like somebody cared about me. Ms. Roberts handed me a tissue. I didn't even know I was crying.

"Shanna, you remind me of myself, you are strong, but you don't realize it. I am expecting great things from you, baby."

When I arrived at Ms. Harris' house, Sonya, from Ms. Seth's house, opened the door.

"What's up Shanna, girl, what you doing here?"

"I'm moving in."

"Cool, I live here."

"What's up Shanna?" It was Sharon, Mrs. Harris' daughter.

"Hey Sharon!" I hugged her tight.

"Shanna was here befo', and my momma been trying to get huh back." Sharon told Sonya.

"I didn't know you stayed here befo'." Sonya was surprised.

"Shanna, momma has four other kids too; they at school now, but you'll see them later. Hell naw, I can't believe my girl is here, and we gonna get fucked up."

I wanted to tell Sharon that I was pregnant, but I didn't want to tell her in front of Sonya. Leonard lived about six blocks away, and I needed to see him. I made an excuse and left Ms. Harris' house alone.

When I got to the store a girl I had never seen was working there.

"Hey, is Leonard around."

"Nope, he don't work here anymore."

I went around back to the house and banged on the door: no lights, and no people. It was clear to me that I was on my own.

The chaos that I used to love at Ms. Harris house got on my nerves that first night. She had too many kids living in an apartment. Somebody was always in the bathroom, and when I did get to it . . . it stunk to high heaven. Being pregnant gave me a sensitive nose. I was happy to be back, but I needed someplace to think, and thinking wasn't happening there because everybody wanted to talk to me.

It wasn't until I got to school the next morning did things slow down. I was in the nurse's office and asked the student worker did they have any information on abortion because I was writing a paper.

She laughed in my face, "Yeah right, at least that is better than you need it for your friend. Look, the school can't have that type of information in here, which is stupid because every day somebody come in here asking for it, here." She gave me the address to a clinic.

Every teacher loaded me up with catch-up work. Some were apprehensive and held back warm greetings, but I understood. I had to prove myself again with them.

I caught the bus to the clinic to get the information. The place was packed, and so many people was talking that I wasn't nervous about asking questions.

"My name is Shashanna Wilson, and I would like to make an appointment."

"For what services?"

"Uh, a abortion."

"How far along are you?"

"Three months."

"What kind of insurance do you have?"

"A medical card."

"Public aid card?"

"Yes."

"Ok."

"How about two weeks from today, will that be okay?"

"Yes."

"You want to be awake or asleep?"

"Do it hurt?" "

"I hear it feels like your monthly menstrual cycle, but it will be a mid-wife there to hold your hand for support."

"Whateva', awake is cool."

"When you get here, you will receive a consultation with an onsite counselor to confirm your decision. Do you have any questions?"

"Uh, Uh."

"You are all set, I'll see you in a couple of weeks."

I was relieved on the bus to Mrs. Harris', and I almost felt like getting high until I had to adjust the school books in my lap. When I was at Mrs. Harris before, Lequisha and I did our homework after school. At her new apartment, there was no one else in the apartment doing homework but me. I had to tell Sharon and Sonya no when they asked me to get high. I was pregnant because I got high and didn't go to school. I was going to the right thing.

I went to the clinic by myself when the day came. I looked around and saw that there were woman and girls who were in my situation, and felt a little less nervous.

"S. Wilson."

I walked through the door and was sent to a counselor who asked me a lot of questions, and she asked me was I sure about my decision. I told her that I was sure, and she gave me options on what birth control to use in the future. Then I was sent to a room where the procedure was to take place.

It was cold, and so was the doctor who performed the surgery. When he began, I interrupted him because I was in pain.

"Do you want to go on with the procedure?" he asked.

"Yes."

"Well, if you keep interrupting me I'm going to have to stop...okay?"

"Okay."

He proceeded, and I interrupted him again.

"Look, I can't continue with this because you are acting like a baby."

"But, you are hurting me."

"Spread your legs and get this over with, it won't take long."

Because of his tone and my urgency to get on with my life, I took the pain, and closed the pregnant chapter of my life.

I was bleeding profusely and had to wear a diaper. I was sent to a recovery room. After a while, a nurse came in and changed my diaper, she gave me an extra one and sent me home.

CHAPTER 25

One Loss After Another

I thought about what Mrs. Roberts said about me being strong. I did feel strong, but I was only strong because I had to be, and that didn't feel right to me. I got C's, D's and one B on my report card. The only person I shared my grades with was Mrs. Roberts, and she sent me a pair of gold plated stud earrings.

I turned seventeen, and that made me old enough to work in the Mayor's summer job program. Getting that job did so much for me; it taught me about working. The idea of working to support myself formed in my mind. The earning of my own money for my own wants and needs felt good. It was like taking my Epilepsy medicine, something I had to do for me. That job made me understand that I had to be responsible for what I wanted and needed.

Once I started making my own money and buying things, I learned that I was responsible for me. My first paycheck made me feel a little grown. I had some money, and since I wasn't getting high, it lasted. The only problem with the money came from my savior, Mrs. Harris.

"Shanna, the agency said that you have to give me some of yo' money to buy your deodorant and keep up with your spending."

"Uh, uh, this is my money, I work for this."

"I'm jus' telling you what they told me."

"They ain't got nothing to do wit' what I spend, no."

Ms. Harris had an attitude with me when I refused, but I didn't want her to be mad, so I gave her ten dollars out of my bi-weekly checks.

For the rest of the summer, I enjoyed getting paid and spending my money on anything that I desired. When school started back, I only had one term of passing grades; I was still a freshman and because I didn't go to summer school I would have had to go to night school, and take classes the upcoming summer to catch up. I should have been going to my junior year, instead I was still a freshman. A seventeen-year-old freshman, that meant I would be twenty, graduating from high school.

The reality of my age and school upset me. I was behind in what I considered the real world, school and working were the real world, and catching up seemed almost impossible until I found out about GED classes. I could take GED classes at the library and take a test that would get me a high school diploma, but the program was only for dropouts. I couldn't be enrolled in high school and take the classes, so I dropped out.

Different people taught the classes at the library: a young college student taught math and science, an older black lady taught reading and English. The books were pamphlets without that much explanation, so I had to go to the classes to understand the work.

What I really liked about the classes was that I was one of the youngest people there; I didn't feel behind taking the classes because most of the people there were grown and had jobs.

The classes were going good then out of nowhere Mrs. Jakes called me at Ms. Harris' house and told me Veronica tried to kill herself and was at the hospital. That shook me to the bone. I dropped the phone and slid to the floor crying. Veronica was good people, a sweet girl who was nice to everybody; why would she try to kill herself? I went in my room and did something I seldom did; I prayed and begged God to help her.

Ms. Harris knocked on my door a little while later and told me, "Shanna, she's gonna be okay now, the hospital released her after they pumped her stomach; she gonna be fine, baby."

Ms. Harris hugged me to assure me that Veronica would be fine. I thanked God and went to sleep.

The next day I walked by Ms. Harris' room, and she was crying.

"What's wrong?"

"Sit down, Shanna. I have something to tell you."

"Oh, no," I started crying again.

Ms. Harris nodded her head to let me know what I was thinking was true.

"Shanna, she's gone. They said that she was fine, but she took some more pills when she got home, and now she's dead."

"Why would they send her back home?"

"They thought she was fine because she told them so."

"She's not dead, no, I don't believe it!"

Ms. Harris reached out to me to embrace me, but I didn't want to be consoled. I shut reality out, and I went to my room and waited for someone to call and say that

Veronica was alive and well. I never got that call. I had to go to a funeral.

Veronica's real family had the nerve to show their faces when she no longer needed them. The agency's staff and other foster mothers came, but I didn't think their grieving was real. I walked past everybody, and I didn't hear a sound. I only knew that I was at Veronica's funeral. When it was time to view the body, I refused to see my friend dead, so I left. I didn't understand why my friend was gone.

I needed to change the way I was feeling, so I got high, no, I got fucked up. I say that because no matter how much weed I smoked or how much beer I drank, I was still thinking about Veronica. Days passed, and I stayed high, but the sadness wouldn't go away. Then something else happened that I didn't see coming.

I started getting into arguments and fights with Ms. Harris and her son, Tom. I overheard Ms. Harris on the phone telling someone that she only buys Tom new clothes, and that she bought us foster kids used clothes. I bought most of my clothes, but what bothered me was that Ms. Harris made a difference between the kids in the house. I didn't think she did that until I heard her say it. I looked at her different after that.

One day, I was in the room with the boys, talking about nothing and laughing. When Tom walked in everyone got quite.

"Why y'all stop talking when I came in here?"

And he started cursing at the sick boy, Joe. I felt it was my duty to defend the kid.

So I told Tom, "Stop picking on him, he wasn't talking about you."

"Shanna, yo' white ass ain't special, you need to shut the fuck up."

"I'm tired of yo' ass walking around here making everybody feel like you better than us, Tom. You ain't." I told him.

"Y'all can't afford clothes like mine because y'all foster kids."

"Bitch, that's our money yo' momma spending on those clothes. If we wasn't here yo' ass would be raggedy."

Tom jumped in my face, and the next thing I knew we were fighting for real. Ms. Harris came into the room and pulled me off of him.

"Get off of my baby." She screamed.

When the fight was over, Ms. Harris and Tom was on one side of the room, and me and the boys were on the other. For some reason, I thought about the fact that Ms. Harris hadn't given me any allowance since the summer, and seeing Tom in a new Adidas outfit pissed me off.

"Can I get my allowance today?"

"You don't do shit around here or go to school, and the agency told me not to give you no allowance."

"I'm taking GED classes, and Ms. Roberts knows that. They didn't tell you to keep my allowance. You can buy yo' son new clothes with our money, and you can't give us our allowance? I heard you on the phone telling somebody that you only buy Tom new clothes."

"You better shut up and mind yo' business."

"You don't have the right to keep our money."

"How you know I ain't giving everybody their money?"

"I know."

"I know you around here getting high, and you betta be careful what chu say to me...okay?"

Right then, I knew that Ms. Harris wasn't any different than any other money grabbing foster mother, and I knew my time at her home was limited.

"Whateva'," I said, and I walked to my room.

I failed my first GED test because I wasn't doing the work at home, and I was barely going to the classes. I needed to do something to change my life. I was leaving the library one afternoon, and I saw a bumper sticker that said, "You can't Sore with Eagles if you Hang with Turkeys." All I knew were turkeys. The only people in my life that wanted to change were in my GED classes; everybody else was happy where they were. I didn't know what I wanted; I just knew I wanted something different.

Tom brought on my last night at Ms. Harris' house. I was feeling bad about failing the GED test, and he was strutting through the house talking about people. He knew I had failed the test.

"How is the dumbest white girl in the country doing?"

I jumped him without saying a word. I started beating him with my fist and didn't stop until Ms. Harris threw me against the wall.

"Leave him alone, what is wrong wit' you?"

When I looked up I saw Tom lying on the floor, and Ms. Harris was trying to revive him. I was afraid because I didn't know what I had done.

"You got to get the fuck out of my house...right now."

"But, he been messing with me, and you didn't do nothing to him."

"I don't care what he said to you. You got to go. Shanna, if you don't get out now, I'm calling the police on you."

I left with nowhere to go.

I rode the busses and el trains all night. The next morning, I called the agency from the library, but Ms. Harris had already contacted them and told them I had a drug problem, and that I was beating on her son. When Ms. Newport came to pick me up, she already had my stuff, so I didn't have to go back to Ms. Harris' place.

CHAPTER 26

Got To Check into Rehab

My next placement totally surprised me. I was expecting to go to another temporary home, but the agency had another idea. I was placed in a drug rehab unit at a hospital.

It wasn't a home; it was a hospital with nurses, counselors, patients, medicine, an intercom system, a dayroom, doctors, rooms, and dope addicts. I instantly hated the place. I only smoked weed and drank beer.

I had to take a physical, meet doctors, and give blood and urine. They acted like I was sick. After they checked me in, I was assigned a room and given a tray with lunch. I sat in the hospital bed and ate. This was different.

A counselor came in and read the rules of the ward to me. She told me I had to obey them. I had an option to leave or comply with the schedule and rules.

I had no place to go, so I told her, "Ok, I will follow the rules." She handed me a blue book. "What is this, a Bible?"

"No, inside there are twelve steps to recovery, and you must commit to them. You must bring this book to all the meetings if you want to stay here."

"I don't want to stay here, but I have to be here."

"If you must be here, you must go by the rules." She said and left.

Later, one of the staff knocked on my door and came into the room. He asked me was I joining the group that was going to be in a few minutes. I refused to answer and turned my head towards the window.

"You are going to have to attend meetings while you are here, like it or not. I'll be by later to let you fill out your menu for dinner and breakfast."

I refused to come out of my room and started flipping the pages of the N.A. book to entertain myself.

He came back and asked, "Do you need help filling out your menu because if you don't specify what you want, they will send you any old thing."

"I'll fill it out, thanks."

"Alright."

I felt exhausted, but I knew I needed to shower from being on busses and trains the night before. Luckily, the shower was in my room. After I showered, I fell asleep and woke up the next morning not knowing where I was then I remembered.

Since I didn't fill out the menu, I got the standard breakfast, oatmeal, toast, and one boiled egg. I ate everything because I was starving.

"Morning meeting, morning meeting," someone was walking through the hall yelling.

I dragged myself out of my room in my hospital gown and footies, and I felt like all eyes were on me.

When I got to the meeting this guy was saying, "Hi, my name is Howard, and I'm an addict."

Everybody talked but me. I went, so I was following the rules.

The Howard guy looked at me and said, "Care to introduce yourself?"

"No."

"Okay, moving right along."

After the morning meeting, I went straight to my room and closed the door. I hadn't made it to my bed before there was another knock on the door.

"Can I come in?"

"What is it?"

"Okay, I'll try another time, see you Wednesday."

Then there was another knock.

"What?"

"Are you going to fill out your menu for lunch?"

I remembered the nasty breakfast I had, so I said, "Yes."

"You'll have to come to the community room to fill it out."

I knew what they were doing. They were trying to make me socialize with the dope addicts.

"Okay, I'll be out."

When I got to the community room, this guy was staring at me, and he was around my age, so I buried my head in the menu. Eventually, he came over and introduced himself.

"I'm Ty, what's yo' name?" I didn't answer Ty and proceeded to fill out my menu. "You don't have to tell me because I already know. Do you smoke squares, Shanna?"

"Yeah."

I needed a square.

"What kind?"

"Benson and Hedges."

"I smoke Newports."

"So."

"I'm jus' trying to be nice and give you some of my squares, bye." I figured I wouldn't be smoking, but he turned around and said, "I don't smoke Benson and Hedges, but here take a Newport."

"Thanks."

"Don't be so evil, smile." I gave Ty a phony smile. "Hey, when my momma visit me this week, I'll give you a pack, okay?"

"Okay."

After I ate a decent lunch, I felt better. I went and watched TV with the other patients, and went to the afternoon group where I introduced myself. It wasn't an NA meeting. People were talking about their families. I didn't have much to say, but I stayed for the whole group.

I had to have a one-on-one with a counselor, and she had some initial questions that got me to thinking; she asked who was important in my life. If she would have asked a week ago, I would have said Ms. Harris, but the only answer I had was Mrs. Roberts. She asked about my mother, and I said no. I didn't even tell her about my brother Carl. I really didn't know who was important to me. I thought about Veronica and got sad. Then I thought about being pregnant and Leonard and got sadder. I wanted to get high right then, so I told her, and she told me to bring it up in group.

No way was I going to talk about that kind of stuff around people I didn't know. When I left the one-on-one

I felt horrible, so I stayed in my room and flipped through the NA book again.

The next morning, I ignored the morning meeting shouts. Then there was a knock on my door.

"Come in."

It was Howard, the NA guy.

"You are not going to feel better sitting in your room." I turned towards the window. He sat on the empty bed that was next to my bed. "It can't be all that bad, what's wrong?"

"Nothing."

"Did somebody die?"

"Not lately."

"Are you about to die?"

"No."

"Then come to group."

When I went, I listened to the dope addicts talking, and some of them wanted to get high too, some of them had lost people they cared about too, some of them had issues with their mothers too, but they were dope addicts, and I only smoked weed and drank beer, so I didn't really talk.

When I had my one-on-one with the counselor, she asked me did I tell the group I wanted to get high.

"No."

"Why not?"

"Because they are real addicts, and I only want to get high to feel better."

"Oh, ok. Well, if you cannot talk about it in the group yet at least write it down in this journal." She handed a book with blank pages and a pen. "I want you to write down every time you think about getting high."

"I will fill the book up in day."

"That's ok, I got plenty more."

She asked me about school, and I told her about dropping out and taking GED classes.

"That's good. Sounds like you are a young lady that makes plans."

She was the first person that told me my dropping was ok since it was part of a plan.

"What are you doing about your plan now?"

I didn't have an answer, and that bothered me. Again, I left the one-on-one feeling worse.

Ty gave me a pack of cigarettes and said we were friends. I almost laughed in his face, but I didn't because he needed a friend. I started spending more time on the unit instead of being in my room, and the groups started to be ok, even the silly ones, like Art. The groups stopped me from thinking about my life and me all the time.

I went to all the morning NA meetings with Howard. I started going because the addicts were talking about changing their lives, which was what I wanted to do. I wasn't a addict, and I couldn't say that I was, but I knew things went better in my life when I didn't get high, and I wanted to change.

Howard started talking to me after the group about not doing drugs anymore. He gave me literature to read and tried to tell me about the steps. But, while he was talking, I would catch him looking at me like a dude and not a counselor. I had a feeling that Howard was beginning to like me, but I ignored the looks because he was so old.

Well, I didn't ignore Howard's interest in me totally, because I would take up the bulk of his time while others had to wait. I thought that I was special, and Howard never complained, but the rest of the staff did, and he had to shorten the time that he spent with me and serve other patients.

I noticed I was writing less getting high thoughts in my journal, and that surprised me. I was doing better with my thinking too. When I thought about my mother I wasn't always mad, and I let myself think about Carl and Veronica. I wasn't an addict, but I did use drugs instead of feeling my pain. I learned that in rehab.

When I had my last one-on-one session, the counselor asked me, "What are you going to do different to stop using drugs?"

Again she made me think.

"I'ma go to the meetings and talk."

I told her what I thought she wanted to hear, but I really didn't know what I was going to do differently. I figured if the agency placed me in a new home I wouldn't be around the same people, and that would help.

It was time for Ty to get released, so at the meeting he got to speak.

"I made friends here, and I learned that I was an addict. I know that I have to go to meetings to stop from using drugs again. The meetings are part of my medicine. I will be able to graduate this year if I stay clean. No, I will graduate this year because I will be clean. I will miss y'all, but I got get back out to the world."

I cried when he left, and he gave me his phone number and told me to call him. When time came for me to leave, I just told everybody goodbye. I never could really talk at the meetings, but I listened a lot and learned some stuff. People signed my NA book, and I got I lot of "I love you" from patients and staff. I sat and waited for my worker and wondered where my next placement would to be.

CHAPTER 27

A Placement That Fits

I was going to be assigned to a different caseworker because of my age, and Mrs. Roberts had gotten a different job. Everything had changed at the agency.

A worker showed me my files and told me point blank it would difficult to place me because of my history. I thought things were looking up after rehab, but she talked to me like I was criminal, and my mood changed.

"There is not much more we can do to do to help you, you got to help yourself at some point."

She made me feel old and unwanted. My files filled up the top of her desk.

"Few homes will take a seventeen year old with your history. I hope you understand that. We have found one home willing to take a chance on you, good luck. Your new worker is out front waiting on you."

I felt rejected until I got in the worker's car, and she was playing one of my jams.

"That's just the way it is, some things will never change, 'cause that's just the way it is."

I don't remember the workers name, but I remember the song that was playing when I met her.

When we arrived to the house this real young lady answered the door and told us to wait. When the same lady came back to unlock the door, I stared at her and thought she was too young to be the foster mother, but she was.

"This is Mrs. Lockwood, your new foster mother, Shanna."

"Hi!"

"If Shashanna gives you any problems call this number, and we'll remove her. Oh, Shashnna needs to get in the GED program because she dropped out of school, and it's mandatory that she starts immediately. Shashanna just got out of a drug rehabilitation center, and she was assigned a sponsor to help her to stay off drugs. He'll be by here once a week to take her to meetings."

The worker spewed out all my business like I wasn't even standing there. If I was foster mom, I wouldn't take me in; I sounded like a problem.

"Okay," then Mrs. Lockwood looked at me. "Anything else I need know?"

"Other than what we told you on the phone and what you have read in the reports, I think that's it." The worker answered.

"You are gonna be okay here, right?" Mrs. Lockwood asked me.

"Yes."

I couldn't get over how young she was and how clean she kept the house.

"You can call me Peaches, everybody else do."

"Okay."

After the worker left, Mrs. Lockwood said, "Let me show you where you gonna sleep."

After I saw the whole house, the song from the car came back into my head. And that song turned out to be the theme song for new placement, different people same bullshit. The front of the house was clean to impress the worker, but the kitchen had roaches and stale food was on the stove. I was thinking, *that's just the way it is. Some things will never change.* But I thought about the addicts at rehab who believed in change, and I had hope.

Mrs. Lockwood was the youngest foster mother I ever had. That was different, and she had the biggest house I ever stayed in, and that was different too, but in the kitchen, I saw empty forty bottles and an empty Tops rolling paper package. That was the same.

When I saw how the rest of the house looked, I knew that this house wasn't strict, and I got worried about getting high. I was very restricted at the rehab, so even if I thought about getting high, it was very unlikely to happen, but this house was different.

"Shashanna, you know this is a new agency that you in?"

"No, I saw changes, but I didn't know it was new."

"Yep, it is still DCFS, but this people don't play. I heard they send kids to juvenile detention that they can't place."

"Is that legal?"

"Baby, you should know by now that this system makes up its own rules. These people do what is easiest for them."

I thought about being made to go to rehab. Even though it helped me, they made me go. I had never heard a foster mother talk against the agency. Peaches was different.

"I'm telling you this because I want you to be careful. Those people ain't your friends, baby."

Peaches had a lot of foster kids staying with her, but she had more space than Ms. Harris, so it didn't feel crowded, and she had three bathrooms. After Peaches finished talking to me, I went in my room and got my journal out. I had been counting my clean days, I was close to sixty days, but I didn't just count my days, I evaluated my thinking about my current situations. I wrote Peaches' name and put a big question mark behind it. She was different, but I didn't know if she a good person; her kitchen had empty forty bottles and an empty package of Tops rolling papers; somebody was getting high.

As I was about to put my journal away, I came across Howard's number, and I smiled.

I went to Peaches and asked, "Can I use your phone?"

"Yea, it's in my room, let me get it."

Like at Mrs. Jakes house, I had to sit right by the bedroom door and talk because of the length of the telephone cord. I dialed each number slowly and anticipated Howard's voice.

"Hello, can I speak to Howard?"

"Hold on. He's not home. Can I take a message?"

"Tell him Shashanna Wilson called."

"Do you have a number where you can be reached?"

"Peaches, what's this number?"

"Who are you giving my number to?"

"My sponsor."

"555-3434"

"555-3434," I repeated.

"Okay, I will let Howard know that you called."

"Okay," I was glad a woman didn't answer.

The next morning, I saw this man coming out of the back bathroom. I wondered where he came from because I didn't see him the day before.

"Hi," he greeted.

"Hi," I answered.

Peaches asked if I was hungry, and I said yes.

"That's my husband."

"Ok." I said, sitting at the kitchen table.

I couldn't identify the breakfast that Peaches had cooked, so I decided not to eat it.

"You never had corn beef hash?"

"What? It looks like dog food."

"Everybody in the house likes it, just try it."

On my plate was the Corn beef hash with an egg, sunny side up, toast, and apple sauce. At first, I was timid about eating the dog food looking stuff, so I ate around it, eating everything else.

"You have to eat it with yo' toast and apple sauce."

Peaches gave me more apple sauce and toast. I started eating the food, and it didn't taste bad. As a matter of fact, I liked it and asked for more. Peaches laughed and gave me seconds.

"What are you going to do about school?"

"I was in a program at the library by my old house. I am going to go back there. I took the test once already and didn't pass, but the teachers said that was alright; I lot of people take it multiple times."

"I heard that too. Well, get right back on the horse. Your worker left you a bus pass."

"Do we get allowance?"

"Yeah."

"How much?"

"A hundred and ten dollars a month."

I wanted to scream because I haven't received that much allowance since I was living with Beth and Carl, and I demanded it.

"What, is something wrong?"

Peaches must have saw the excitement on my face.

"Uh,uh. Do I have to buy my clothes and other stuff with it?"

"If you mean soap, deodorant, and toilet tissue, no, I buy those things."

I noticed that every kid in the place, including the older girls, were a little weird, so I asked, "Those other girls, what's wrong wit' them?"

"This is a specialized home, that's why you here."

"Me?" Wasn't nothing wrong with me.

"You have seizures, right?"

"Yeah, that reminds me I have to take my medicine."

"One of those other girls has seizures too. What kind do you have?"

I was totally oblivious to the fact that I stayed in a specialized foster home with mentally challenged and alcohol syndrome kids. I was considered specialized because I had Epilepsy, which I didn't understand because my illness didn't require special care. I didn't have to get on the short yellow school bus nor did anyone have to administer medication to me.

"The ones when I pass out…grand mal…something like that."

"Those are serious, be sure you keep up with your medicine. Do you talk to your real mother?"

"Yes."

"Do you ever want to stay with her?"

"No, and I don't want to talk about her. Can I have some more hash stuff?"

She gave me the last of it.

"You ever eat meatloaf?"

"Yeah, but I don't like it."

"You gonna like mine, watch."

After breakfast, I went back to my room, got my journal and put a real big smiley face behind Peaches' name.

"Shashanna, the phone!"

I went and got it, wondering who could be calling me. I hoped it wasn't my mother. I wasn't ready for her drama and disappointments, not yet.

"Hello?"

"Hey, Shanna, this is Howard, you okay?"

"Oh yeah, I forgot I called you. When can we go to a meeting?"

"I have to ask the new foster mother first. Let me speak to her."

"Okay."

I passed the phone to Peaches.

"Hi, I'm Shashanna's foster mother, Peaches. Who are you? Howard? Are you her sponsor? Ok. Tonight, what time? You have to have back before curfew. Eleven o'clock. Okay."

Peaches gave me back the phone.

"Pick you up at six."

I was grinning from ear to ear when I got off the phone, so much so that Peaches said, "He sounds like he's older than I am. Are you sure he's not up to something besides sponsoring you?"

"No, he jus' trying to keep me clean."

"Yeah, ok. Be careful, a man is still a man, and most men are only out for one thing, and it's not trying to keep you drug free."

"Howard's cool. He won't do that."

I went through the NA Basic Text while I waited for six o'clock and Howard. He was on time, but he didn't have a car.

"You don't have a car?"

"Oh, I forgot to tell you, but I have bus fare for the both of us."

"I thought since you a counselor you would have a car."

"My car is in the shop being repaired."

"Oh, okay."

The meeting was another disappointment. Since I didn't know the people, they all sounded like they were whining. After the meeting, we stopped for a bite to eat.

"I hope you haven't did any drugs?"

"Nope, I been clean."

"Good."

"You know I just smoked weed anyway."

"Shanna, weed is a drug, and if you smoked it when you didn't want to, you are an addict."

"No, I'm not."

"Ok."

"I'm not."

I didn't say it when I was in rehab, and I wasn't saying it on the outside. Howard gave me a look, a dude to girl look, and I ignored it.

"It's time for you to take me back home. I jus' got there, and I don't want to mess it up."

He got me home and waited at the door until Peaches opened it. When I got in the house, Peaches asked me a ton of questions, and I reassured her that everything was fine between Howard and me.

"Shashanna, how old is that man?"

"I don't know, you asked me that befo'."

"Yes, but it's something about him that's sneaky. I don't trust him. You are a pretty young lady, and men will try to take advantage of you."

"He is my sponsor, Peaches."

"Okay, if you say so."

For the next meeting, Howard had his car, and instead of going to NA meeting, he suggested we hang out and talk. We got some chicken and ate it sitting on the truck of his car, looking up at the stars. He had some old folk's music playing on the radio.

"Don't you like this song, Shanna?"

"Nope." Howard turned the volume up and told me to listen close. "Nope, I still don't like it."

"I love this song. They singing about how I feel about you."

I understood enough of the song to know it was a love song.

"Huh?"

Then Howard took me in his arms and started dancing, and he kissed my neck. I pulled away. I started to tell him to take me home right then, but I was hoping I was reading him wrong.

"You know, I think we can still make a meeting," he said, looking down at his watch.

"Good," I said, because we didn't need any more alone time.

"There's an NA meeting close by here at the C and H motel."

"Why is it at the motel?"

"Because it's the only place that gave them a free room."

"Oh, okay."

When we got to the Motel, I had to wait until Howard come out of the office of the motel.

"We over here in this room." When he opened the door, there was no one inside. "I guess they haven't arrived yet, but they'll be here soon."

I looked at Howard and said, "I got to go."

"Take off your shoes and get comfortable, you look tense. Can I give you a massage?"

"Naw, I'm okay."

"Turn the TV on while we wait for everybody else."

"Nope, I got to go."

"Come closer."

"I'm fine. Where is everybody else at?"

"It's just gone be me and you."

Peaches was right. Howard was just another nasty man.

"Take me home, or I'm going to start screaming."

"What?"

"I said, I want your old ass to take me home before I start screaming rape."

"You serious?" He said, blinking his eyes like he had a tic.

"Peaches told me not to trust you, but I told her you was my sponsor, and all you wanted to do was help me stay clean."

I started crying because his old ass hurt my feelings. Yeah, we flirted with each other in rehab, but I didn't think he really wanted to have sex with me.

"I thought you was my sponsor," I cried, "You was supposed to help me, not fuck me. Take me home."

And he did, I never saw Howard again, but he fucked me up good. He made stop believing in everything I learned at rehab. In my head, all I heard was, *That's just the way it is, some things will never change, 'cause that's just the way it is.*

When I got back to Peaches', I tore up my journal and threw my NA basic text away.

CHAPTER 28

Temptation VS. Strength

The next morning part of me wanted to get high, but a bigger part didn't. I caught the bus back to the library, and both GED teachers were there. I got back in to the classes. I went all month without missing a class. One of the ladies taking the class worked at a doughnut place downtown, and she said they were hiring.

I couldn't wait to get home to tell Peaches, but when I walked in the phone rang, and it was for me. It was my worker, they had arranged a meeting with my mother, me, and Carl while I was in rehab, and they forgot to tell me when I got out; the meeting was that afternoon, and she was on her way to pick me up. I was going to get see Carl. I hung up the phone with tears forming in my eyes.

"What's wrong, Shanna?" Peaches asked.

"Nothing, I'm going to see my mother and my brother."

It was small meeting room at the agency. The same worker that took me to Peaches' house picked me up and set up the room. I was the first one to get there, so I sat at the table waiting for my mother and my brother. Carl walked through the door first with my mother right behind him. I jumped up and hugged him.

"Man, I'm glad to see you, where you been?"

"I moved back with Beth." He said.

I thought I heard him wrong, "Really?"

"Yeah, it ain't like it was though."

He looked almost the same except for few scars on his face. My mother looked bad, her cheeks were sunken in and she had dark circles under her eyes. She looked worse than the addicts at the rehab.

"That bitch took y'all from me. Where she at so I can kill huh?"

"Mom, be glad that me, you and Shanna is here now." Carl said, smiling big at me.

He had lost a tooth on the side.

"I remember when she put that hand print on Shanna's face, and that's why I reported huh ass. Has that bitch been hitting you too, Carl?"

"Momma, that was the past." He said.

"I still hate huh ass, and I'll still have y'all if she didn't take my babies."

I looked at Carl, and he looked at me because we knew exactly what happened to us, and Beth wasn't the blame. We all sat at the table, me and Carl on one side, our mother on the other.

"Lil sis, where you stay at now?"

"On the Southside."

"This is the Southside."

"Way south."

"I tell you what, give me yo' numba, and I'll come over to visit. I can visit you, right?"

"I have to ask Peaches, my foster mother, but I'll give you da numba."

"Shashanna, are you in school?" My mother asked.

"I'm taking GED classes."

"Good, a lot of folks getting their GEDs. I am happy you trying to do something wit yo' life," she said, as she reached across the table and held my hand.

I wanted to pull away, but I didn't.

We all talked around the past, which was cool because I didn't want to get mad. I wanted to ask Carl did he have any more kids, but I didn't because I felt like I should have known that. I knew we would catch up a little bit at a time. My mother pulled out two pictures of herself for me and Carl to take with us. I thought that was funny, but again, I kept my opinion to myself. The worker came in and set up another meeting for the following month. We all agreed.

I wanted a new outfit to wear downtown to fill out the application, so I asked Peaches for my allowance.

"They haven't paid me for you yet. When the pay me I will give it to you. I guess since they a new agency they behind a little."

She didn't look me in face when she said it. Peaches always looked me in my face when she talked to me.

"Ok." I said.

The lady from the GED class hooked me up, and I got the job right away, and I met a cute boy when I got off the bus.

"What's yo' name?"

"Shashanna."

"I'm Jr., but you can call me Taye, my real name."

I stared at Taye because he was so fine, and his smile made me melt.

"I know you smoke weed, wanna smoke a joint?"

"Yea." I said without even thinking.

"Where were you coming from?"

"I just got a job downtown."

We had walked a couple of blocks then Taye said, "I live here." He pointed to a red brick house. "We can go up to my room and smoke this joint."

"Cool."

It was just a joint, and he was so fine.

His room was right before the kitchen. As soon as he closed his bedroom door, we started kissing and off came our clothes and we started having sex. And it wasn't just a couple of seconds, we did it a long time, and we kept kissing all while we was doing it. I was acting like a ho, and I knew it.

It was our first time together, and we was fucking like we was married. After he came, he didn't go to sleep. We smoked the joint then we did it again, and again, and it felt real good every time. I was finally having sex.

"Girl, you something else you know that?"

I smiled and was glad that Taye liked my company. It looked like he shared his room with someone else, so I began to put my clothes back on.

"Relax, my brother won't be here for a while, and my mother is at work. I can't wait for you to meet my mom, she gonna like you."

I didn't know if I wanted to meet his mother. But, I knew I wanted to have some more sex, and we did.

"Since you know where I stay, come by."

Nope, it wasn't going to go like that.

"Here is my number, you can call me. I be going to GED classes, and I just got a new job. I want to see you again, but I can't just be hanging out."

He looked puzzled. Taye made me feel secure, and I didn't have to think twice about him liking me, but I was not about to spend my days in his room; I had already done that.

"What school you go to?" I asked him.

"I dropped out last year."

"Oh," I didn't say anything else.

After I left Taye's house, I couldn't stop smiling: a new job and a new boyfriend all in one day. If I would have still had my journal, I would have wrote his name with a big smile behind it.

I got along ok with the other girls at Peaches' house, but they were doing stuff I had done. I thought about my last one-on-one at rehab; she asked me what was I gonna do that was different: getting a job was different, and going to GED classes for a month straight and doing the home work was different, smoking a joint was the same, but having good sex was different. I decided I was doing ok.

I started working downtown for three dollars and thirty-five cents an hour. I made ninety- five dollars bi-weekly before taxes. It wasn't a lot of money, but it was all mine. I got off one night and I was catching the el home and I suddenly felt dizzy, but I ignored it until I felt myself getting weak. I sat down, and that was the last thing I remembered.

I woke up in a stranger's house on a mattress on the floor. There was a lady standing over me, and a man sitting at a table.

"You okay? You had a seizure on the el', so I took you home wit' me. I went through yo' wallet and called someone, and they gonna be here to pick you up. Here is a glass of water. You is lucky that you wasn't on the el' platform. You could have fallen in front of the train."

The worker came with the police, and they drove me back to Peaches'. With working, going to classes, and being with Taye, I had slipped up on taking my medicine. But the lady was right. I could have passed out in front of a train and died.

Enough time had passed for Peaches to get paid from the agency. I had been paid twice from my job, and the little checks weren't going far enough especially since I was back to smoking weed with Taye, and he never had any real money, only enough to buy a couple of joints.

"Peaches, can I get my allowance?" I asked while she was cooking dinner one night.

"Nope, they still ain't sent me your check yet."

I had been in her house over three months. I knew she was lying.

"I'ma call the agency and see what's up, they should have sent it to by now."

"Wait a couple more days, no sense in getting them all riled up."

The next day she gave me my allowance. They was all the same, no matter how nice they acted, every foster mother was money hungry.

I liked Taye, but I was getting tired of spending my money on him. He was always broke, and if we did anything, even went to Wendy's, I had to pay for it. Then I met this other dude, a friend of Peaches' husband, and he was different.

Willie was older than me, but younger than Peaches' husband. We had seen each other at the house but didn't do anything but smile at each other. Then one day, again getting off the bus, he pulled up on me in his Chevy.

"What's up, girl? Get in."

The car smelled like weed, but he wasn't smoking. I felt nervous because he was a grown man, and I knew I wanted to get with him. He had muscles on top of muscles, and I could see the print of his dick in his jeans. He turned me on from looking at him.

"Where you know Peaches' husband from?"

"We were in the penitentiary together; I just got out last week."

"You what?"

"K-rod never told you that?"

"K-rod?"

"You didn't know his name?"

"Naw, because he is always in da room wit da doe closed."

"He ain't long got out himself."

"What."

"Yeah, he was sentenced fuh twenty years."

"What? What chu was in fuh, Willie?"

"Something I didn't do, and I don't want to talk about it."

"Okay."

"Let's go to my place."

He wasn't asking, so I didn't bother to answer. I would have did it with him right there in the car, I wanted him that bad. It was funny; after me and Taye really did it, I wanted to do it all the time, and I started wanting to do it with more than Taye.

As soon as we walked into his apartment, the phone rang. It was Peaches calling for me. So Willie handed me the phone.

"You ain't fucking that man is you, Shanna?"

"No."

"He ain't trying nothing wit you is he?"

"No, we jus' talking."

"Shanna, I want you to come home, and I mean right now."

"Ok," I hung up.
"How she know I was over?" I asked Willie.
"K-rod told me where you get off the bus; he must have told her."

When I got home, Peaches let me have it, "I ain't going to jail because your young ass is hot. After you turn eighteen and your ass ain't living here, you can fuck whoever you want, but now, in this house, stay your ass away from grown ass men."

Willie and me never hooked back up, but it was like Peaches said, I guess. I was hot, and I ended up hooking up with a couple guys in the hood, and it was cool, but I knew things weren't going the way I wanted because I got bored with them so fast. Then I met this guy named Ray, Taye's cousin, a big time dope dealer in the hood.

I had just got off work, and I was carrying a Foot Locker bag with a new pair of Nikes.

"What's in the bag?"
"Why?"
"Looks like it's getting heavy."
I stopped and laughed.
"You Shanna, you be over my cousin Taye's house."
"Yeah."
"I'm Ray."
"I know."
"So you know me?"
"I know of you," and my brain was saying "stay away."
"Come go wit' me."
I got into his car.
"Where we going?"
"Relax, I got something to do then we can chill."

I liked his confidence; we pulled up in front of a house and went in. He had keys like it was his house. None of the dudes I had kicked it with had a house.

"Who live here, Troy?"

"This lady let me hold down her spot to bag my product."

"Product?"

All of a sudden, Troy pulled out this big freezer zip lock bag full of cocaine and poured it on a mirror. I became silent because I never seen so much cocaine, and I was worried about the police busting in on us.

"You okay?" He asked.

"Yeah."

"Why you quite then?"

"Is da door lock?"

"Yeah, ain't nobody coming in here."

"You sure?"

"Shanna."

"Okay."

Troy pulled out this jar and filled it half way with water and poured the cocaine in it and then he boiled the water until the cocaine became rock and poured it out. I thought to myself, *he could be a scientist or something; that was magic.*

"How you do that?"

"I mix baking soda water and the product together, and it makes a rock after I cook it."

For some reason, my attraction to Troy grew stronger. Maybe he had some sort of power because suddenly he got finer.

"You want a piece of this?"

"I don't do cocaine."

"Here jus' take this wit' you. You can sell it or whateva'."

"Okay."

"You got some weed, Troy?"

"Yea, let me call my boy, Mike, he got some."

When Troy's boy came with the weed, I asked him for some tops.

"You eva put some rock on yo' weed?"

"Nope. Is that how you smoke yo' weed, Mike?"

"Yea, try it."

Mike passed me a joint with rock cocaine in it, and I smoked it.

"Damn, this shit feels real good."

I knew I was going to have a problem with weed and cocaine mixed, primos, because I smoked the rock that Troy gave me with my weed. Then I had an idea.

"Troy, since I know everybody around here, I can sell some of yo' product."

"I don't know, Shanna."

"Come on. Give me ten bags, and we'll go from there."

"You sure?"

"Troy, come on."

"Here girl, they ten dollars apiece, bring me back seventy."

"Okay."

Troy was so nice; it was hard to believe that he was a big time drug boy in the hood. We didn't get sexual that day, but we established a business relationship. I never made a profit, in the beginning, but I always had his money. I would sell a few bags and smoke the rest. Eventually, I stopped putting it on weed and smoked in a pipe.

One day when I went back to Troy to cop, he asked me, "Are you smoking this stuff?"

"Why you say that."

"Cuz you tweaking!"

"Tweaking?"

"Yeah, you all hyped up."

"Just give me ten more."

"Alright."

CHAPTER 29

Legally A Woman (Mistake Number Two)

I figured I had went to enough classes and did enough work to try the GED test again. The teachers told me I wasn't ready, but I was high on rock all the time, so I didn't listen. I took the test, and I failed again. That bummed me out, so I stopped going to the classes.

My birthday came and I was turning eighteen, and I was finally turning a profit from selling Troy's rocks, so I decided to go out and have a real good time.

Eighteen meant a lot, I was grown. I wanted to spend the day with someone special, so I chose Troy.

"Whose birthday is it today?" I asked him.

"Don't play. Ya know I already know. What chu doing today?"

"I wanna kick it wit chu."

"Okay, you need some money to buy you something?"

"Yeah, I'm gonna buy a mini dress, so you can see me in it."

"Hell yea, here's thirty dollars."

"I'm going shopping."

"You coming back later?"

"Yeah."

I bought this red and black striped mini-mini dress. I looked good in it. I went back to the house and took a shower and maneuvered my way into the tight dress then I let my hair down.

"You going out hoeing? Where is the rest of yo' clothes?"

Peaches and I were ok, but we weren't cool anymore. I was never at the house. Between working, the classes, selling Troy's product, and my own partying, we hardly saw each other.

"Peaches, this is a dress, it's not that short, is it?"

"Y'all girls these days got tiddy's and ass for days...jus' be careful out there."

I thought, *I must be looking good for Peaches' to say that.* I couldn't wait to see Troy's reaction.

Taye and me had stopped kicking it because he was always broke. Troy had moved into the basement of his house, so I saw Taye from time to time. I saw him on my birthday.

"Where you going in that dress?" Taye was looking out of the window.

"It's my birthday."

"Well Happy Birthday, baby."

"Thanks."

Taye closed his window, and I proceeded to ring Troy's bell. Troy always met me at his front door, as if he was being discreet about my visits.

"Hey Troy, you like?"

"Damn, let's walk around the corner. You bought that with the money I gave you?"

"Yep."

"I'll buy you another cuz you look good, turn around and let me see all of you."

I modeled the dress as Troy's jaw dropped. When cars were stopped and guys looked at me, Troy stepped in front of me to cover me up.

"You jealous?" I asked.

"Naw, I'm jus' protecting you. You is drawing a lot of attention on yo'self."

"You like the dress or not?"

"Yeah, girl."

"So what's up with us on my birthday?"

"You know what? Come on, let's go to a hotel."

"Foreal?"

"Yeah, it's that time."

We both were excited; we hadn't did the sex thing yet. We made money together, but we had yet to cross over to the real deal. I wanted him bad, but as a baller, Troy had a lot of women.

The hotel had a lounge, so we went there first. Troy didn't drink, but he bought me one because it was my birthday. When we got to the room he gave me some coke to put on my weed, and the mood was right. My plan was to make Troy come back for more. Troy pulled off his pants, and I looked, and looked again. I figured he wasn't hard all the way, but he got on top of me, he gave it all to me, and I wanted more. I didn't think about a condom, but I should have.

Weeks later, after missing my period, I thought, *it is always the little ones*. I was pregnant again, and it was time for my six month evaluation with the agency.

Peaches and I were no longer cool. My job was only giving me ten hours and I was barely showing up for those and I wasn't going to the GED classes and the man I thought was so much was so little. It wasn't a good time in my life.

After the statement of my history, which I hear at every evaluation, the worker would ask the foster mother how I was doing. I had had a couple of good ones with Peaches. I wasn't expecting a good one this time, but I was eighteen; things were different.

"Mrs. Lockwood, how is Shashanna doing in your home?"
"Well, Shanna is never home, and I ask her all the time about getting her GED, but she don't listen."
"I see. Is Shashanna maintaining her sobriety as stated in our records?"
"I really don't know. Shashanna, you doing drugs?"
"Yep," I answered because I was always honest during the evaluations.
"Mrs. Lockwood, would you say that Shashanna gets along with the other children in your household, and does she obey your household rules?"
"Like I said, Shanna is never home, and she has a mind of her own."
"Shashanna, what are your plans for the next six months?"
"To get my GED."
"You were supposed to work on getting your GED eight months ago, what is your reason for not doing so?"
"Lazy, I have no excuse."
The DCFS worker was stunned by my candor.
"She always tells the truth, no matter what," Peaches said.
"We have given you numerous opportunities to get yourself together, Shashanna. You are eighteen years old, and we can discontinue your case because you are legally grown. Unless you decide get yourself together while in

Mrs. Lockwood's home, we will have no choice but to discontinue services. Are we clear on your goals?"

"Yes, get my GED and obey Mrs. Lockwood's household rules."

"Mrs. Lockwood, are you willing to keep Shashanna in your home and work with her?"

"As long as she do as she is told, I have no problem with her living with me."

I had other plans.

When I got back to the hood, I tracked Troy down. I made up my mind to tell Troy that I was pregnant, and I wanted an abortion.

I found him in the basement of Taye's house. He didn't want to talk there so we meet at the park.

"I'm pregnant, and I want to have an abortion."

He ignored what I said and asked about his money from the rocks.

"You have my money?"

"Yeah, Troy."

"Give it to me."

I handed him his seventy dollars.

"You been acting strange with me, Shanna."

"Troy, I'm pregnant."

"What chu mean?"

"Pregnant, I'm fixin' to have your baby."

"I haven't seen you for a while, and we ain't fucked but one time."

"I'm pregnant…by you."

"How you know its mines?"

"Damn Troy."

"I'm jus' sayin'!"

"Sayin' what?"

"You know how you is. I'm not the only one you be kicking it wit'."

"Troy, it's yours. I used protection with everybody else."

"How I know that?"

"Look, give me the money for the abortion, I don't want this baby."

"You want an abortion?"

"Yeah, you ain't my man."

"I tell you what, come back later, and I'll have the money fuh you."

I had heard those words before. Troy was going to play me, and I knew it. I didn't even go back. I had a medical card.

"Fuck Troy," I said to the wind and went home.

Again, I went to the clinic by myself and did what I had to do. The abortion wiped me out again mentally and physically. I was tired of everything and everybody.

I didn't want to get high, I didn't want to go to classes, and I sure as hell didn't want to hear shit from Peaches or a DCFS worker. I got fired from the job, so I didn't have shit to do but sit around the house and mope. Peaches said I needed a counselor.

I told her, "Get the fuck out of my face."

She called DCFS. I didn't give a fuck. I was tired of me and my life. I didn't think I could change, and I didn't want the life I had. When the DCFS worker came to pick me up, I told her, "Fuck you too, I ain't leaving."

She called the police, and they took me from Peaches' home.

CHAPTER 30

Got To Check into Rehab, Again

They took me back to rehab, and this time I was cool with being there. I was away from everybody and everything. When I looked in the mirror I saw black circles under my eyes, my cheeks had sunken in and I saw the scars and scratches from my past fights. The face I saw in the mirror looked like a dope addict.

I got there in the afternoon, and again, I had to have a physical. I tested positive for cocaine, marijuana, gonorrhea, a yeast infection and I had crabs. My blood count was low, and I had no Epilepsy medicine in my system. The nurse couldn't believe that they allowed me to have an abortion in my physical condition. They put me on an I.V. and bed rest. I couldn't attend any meetings for three days.

When the nurse asked me had I thought about killing myself, I said, "No, but I wouldn't mind dying." That got me scheduled for psychiatrist. I didn't care. At the very first meeting I attend, I told them, "Hello, my name Shanna, and I am addict."

Howard didn't work there anymore, and I wasn't surprised. They gave me another NA Basic Text, a journal and a Just for Today daily meditation book. The lady that had Howard's job asked me did I think I was powerless over drugs and alcohol.

I had to think about that, but after a day or so I told her yes because I used drugs when I didn't want to, and drugs stopped me from doing what I wanted to do with my life.

"Congratulations, you completed Step One."

I didn't know I had to complete steps. I guess Howard was too busy trying to get into my pants to really tell me about the program, or maybe he did, and I didn't hear him. Whatever the staff asked me to do, I did. I worked in my journal, did my step work, went to all the meetings and I started praying, all the time.

When I was admitted, my mother somehow got listed as my next of kin, and they contacted her for family day. I went along with it because I willing to do whatever it took to change and get better.

But as soon as she walked on the unit, I got angry. I couldn't do a family session with her, so the counselor suggested she stay for the NA meeting. I had been talking in the meetings because I felt everyone was being honest. My mom was a bull-shitter.

Instead of saying her name and she was an addict, she said, "Hello, I am Shanna's mother, and I am here to help her and be supportive any way I can. Shanna, why don't you stand up and say something?" I just looked at her. "Shanna, you need to say something, they just trying to help you."

The guy who was chairing the meeting said, "This meeting is for addicts only." He looked at my mom and asked, "are you an addict?"

That was the million dollar question.

"What?"

"Are you and addict?"

"This is about my daughter, not me."

"No, this is a meeting for addicts, not just your daughter. Every addict here benefits from this meeting. Are you an addict?"

My mother got up and stormed out.

I ignored her leaving and said, "My name is Shanna, and I am an addict working on Step Two. I would like to hear how others came to believe that a power greater than themselves could restore them to sanity."

My mother never visited me in rehab again, and I was more than grateful. When time came for me to leave, I had forty-two clean days and I was working on step three and I really didn't want to go. I felt safe in rehab, protected from drugs and myself.

I was told by DCFS that I had exhausted all possibilities for placement in any foster care agency. My worker gave my mother a call to ask her could I stay with her. I guess at this point DCFS didn't care if my mother was engaging in drugs or not, I was eighteen. Being eighteen meant that I was grown and wasn't considered to be anyone's responsibility.

I was worried, no, I was scared. All I had was forty-two days and a belief in a power greater than myself. My mom came and picked me up, along with her dirty old ass boyfriend, who was glad that I was moving in with them.

"Shanna, just because you gonna stay with me doesn't mean you can do what chu wanna do." My mother said with a stern voice.

I looked at my mother and said, "Ok."

When we got there I was escorted to the guest room and didn't come out except to use the bathroom. I was trying to get centered in my mind and not be angry about my situation. I thought about what Peaches said about the agency, these people do what they want to do. I had just gotten out of rehab, and they sent me to live with my mom, who had a known drug history.

My mom acted like I needed her, and I guess I did, but she treated me like I was some stranger on the street that she let stay in her home. She knew she was my last resort, and I was reminded of it over and over.

She was standing in the doorway of my bedroom when she said, "Shanna, you can't stay in the room all day every day. You act like I'm supposed to let you stay in my house. DCFS didn't want you because you are a problem and your attitude is funky."

"Mom, why are you saying this to me? I didn't say nothing to you."

"That's yo' problem, you don't respect me."

"Please, leave me alone."

I was trying to stay clean and serine, but my mother's home was filled with arguments and confusion. If I wanted to stay clean I had to leave, but the agency made it clear that didn't have any other placement for me, but I called them anyway.

I was assigned to a new worker…a male. His name was Mr. Charles. I told him about my situation at my mother's house, and he told me he was coming over the next day.

Mr. Charles did a home inspection and interviewed me and my mother.

"What's yo' name any way Mr.?" My mom asked.

"My name is Mr. Charles. Shanna's assigned worker."

"Well, she need to talk to somebody because her attitude is bad. Will you talk to huh?"

She talked about me as if I wasn't sitting right in front of her.

"Yes ma'am, I'll talk to her."

Mr. Charles looked at me with pity in his eyes.

To my mother he said, "Ms. Wilson, will you give Shashanna and I some privacy?"

"Awh, why?"

"Ms. Wilson, please."

"Alright," my mom was offended, but she left us in the living room alone.

"Shashanna when wards like you get a certain age, foster care placement is no longer an option."

"What?"

"It is time for you to get your own apartment. I believe your sobriety is at risk here. I'm going to work on it right away, but there is a process so hang in there."

I was oblivious to what the process was, but it didn't matter, as long as I was away from my mother.

The process started with me going to court. Mr. Charles picked me up a week later and drove me downtown to the court building. He explained that the way process worked was that I would have to refuse to sign release papers and stay in the care of DCFS. He talked as if he was telling me a secret.

He couldn't go into the courtroom with me, but he hugged me tight and said, "Good luck Ms. Wilson."

I was sitting in the court room, and short a fat lady approached me.

"Are you Shashanna Wilson?"

"Yes."

"I'm your legal advisor. I will be representing you. DCFS wants you to sign some papers to release you from their guardianship because you are legally considered an adult. You have a right to not sign the papers, and they'll have to place you in a facility until you are twenty one."

Mr. Charles had explained this, but her words still confused me, so I took breath and asked, "What do that mean?"

"Look, if you sign the papers for DCFS to terminate you, you are free to go. And if you don't, you will be in the custody of DCFS until you are twenty-one, which means they will have to place you in a program called independent living."

"Independent living?"

"You will have your own apartment at the expense of DCFS until you turn twenty-one."

"Awh, so don't sign the papers?"

"I can't make any decisions for you; you have to make them for yourself." They lady said with her glasses on the tip of her nose, looking down to me.

"Case number one, DCFS vs. Shashanna Wilson. Are both parties present?"

We stood and walked up to the judge.

"Yes," my legal advisor answered.

"Yes." The people from DCFS answered.

"I understand that DCFS no longer wants custody of the defendant, Shashanna Wilson, because she had exhausted all of her placements in foster care. Is that correct?"

"Yes Sir."

"Ms. Wilson, will you step up to the podium?" I walked toward the judge, and he looked at me with

concern in his eyes. "Young lady, do you wish to sign over your rights to DCFS as your legal guardian?"
"No, I'm not signing no papers."
"Ok, Court is adjourned."
I had to be placed in a group home that same day.

CHAPTER 31

Independence

I had to wait all day for DCFS to find placement and assign a new worker, Ms. Clades. She placed me in two group homes, and each was filled with drama, but I stayed out of it. I had a long term plan to get my own place.

I went to GED classes at different facilities, and I kept going to NA meetings when I could. I didn't have a sponsor, but through the meetings I was able to keep up with my step work. Things weren't easy, but I had a plan, and I truly believed that a power greater than myself was working with me.

My biggest problem at both group homes was staying out of the drama. I was scared of getting high, but sometimes I got bored and wanted to be involved in some mess, and there was plenty of it around. What saved me was remembering.

Whenever I thought about getting into it with somebody, I thought about living with my mom, or I thought about my abortions, or I thought about being the hospital with gonorrhea and crabs, or I thought about how Leonard and Troy dogged me out, and then I would think about my mother and how easy it would be for me to end up like her. I didn't want to be a person who lived life lying to themselves. I was doing good, and I knew it. All I had to do was keep doing good.

I was at my second group home placement when I got a call that affirmed I was doing right.

"Shashnna you have a phone call."
"Where at?"
"In the office."
"Okay."
"Hello."
"Pack your bags!"
"Who is this?"
"Ms. Clades, now pack your bags."
"Where I'm going this time?"
"You finally are getting what you want."
"You playing?"
"No, pack your bags."

I thanked her, and thanked her again, but I remembered Mr. Charles. If he hadn't gone that extra mile with me when I was staying with my mother, I wouldn't have had a plan.

I didn't have much to pack up; half a plastic bag of clothes and a bunch of gratitude.

Ms. Clades picked me up from the group home and took me to the Independence for Youth agency. I met the director of the agency and a social worker.

"Hi my name is Linda, and I'll be your social worker, and may I say that you are so pretty, ever think about modeling?"

I looked at Ms. Clades and smiled and said, "No."

Linda spoke with an accent and wore glasses.

"Shashanna, are you ready to have your own place?" She asked.
"Yes, I'm ready. Right, Ms. Clades?"
"Yes, she is ready." Ms. Clades smiled.
"We have rules and regulations just like everywhere else. We give a forty-dollar allowance every week, and we have meetings every Wednesday that are mandatory. From time to time, we inspect your apartment to see how well it's maintained. We also, have counselors who will assist you with looking for employment and your educational goals. Shashanna, do you have any?"
"I want to get my GED, who do I talk to?"
"We'll assign you to a counselor who will have information about GED sites near you."
"Okay."
"This agency is a part of DCFS, and your rent is covered until you turn twenty-one. Now, where would you like to stay? We have apartments available on the north side and south side."
I wanted different, no, I needed different. I wasn't going back to the hood.
"The north side, I wanna stay up north."
"Are you sure?"
"Yes."
My old neighborhood had old problems and old traps.
"Okay, we have a place for you, but it is unfurnished for now. We will get you basics over the next couple of days."
"That's okay; I can sleep on da flo'!"
"For now, we'll get you some padding to lay on tonight."

On our ride to my apartment, we took Lake Shore Drive, and I had never seen this part of Chicago in my life. It was a new beginning, and I felt like I was starting over in life.

"Shashanna, in this building there is a laundry facility, so you don't have to go to a Laundromat to wash. We are here."

"Already?"

As we got out of the car, I looked around and saw lots of trees and no one was hanging on the corners or in front of any houses. The entire block was quite, and the snow made it look like Christmas.

"You are on the first floor apt. 1E, to your right."

Linda handed me the key, and I turned the key to my apartment. The studio apartment was huge.

"We have to get this old couch out of here when we bring your furniture tomorrow."

"You like it?"

"I love it."

Linda sat and talked to me for a little while, but I wasn't listening. I was overwhelmed with joy.

"Okay, I'll see you tomorrow and take you to get some furniture for your new apartment."

"Okay, okay!"

"See you tomorrow."

I closed the door and sat on the old couch and cried because I was so happy.

I enjoyed waking up in my own place not hearing a sound other than mine. I showered and walked my place naked. I didn't rush to dress because the sun wasn't up yet. My window faced the brick wall of the building next door, but that was ok with me. Everything was ok with me. I finally got dressed and went to the nearest grocery store for some food.

Later, Linda came by as promised and took me furniture shopping. I got a new bed and love seat and other things that I needed from the resale store. I was happy.

After we bought the furniture, she took me back to the agency, so I could meet with my counselor and set up my GED classes and talk about a job. I didn't mention NA meetings to her because I didn't want her to think I had a drug problem. I didn't know how much she knew about me.

My workers name was Terrance, and he was fine with a big "juicy" butt. I hadn't had sex in while, and that was the first thing that came into my mind when I saw him.

During our initial meeting, Terrance was more interested in finding me a job than getting me set up GED classes. I was disappointed, but I followed his lead and took down the information he gave me. He was all business, but I had a feeling he would come around later. After I got all the job leads, I asked about the GED classes.

"Terrence, do you know where I can take some GED classes?"

"No, but the next time you come in I'll have some information for you."

"Thanks Terrance."

He stood and walked me to the door, and damn, I wanted to grab a hold of his big juicy butt.

I went to the employment agency Terrence sent to me, but there was more to it than he explained. I waited so long that when they did call me, the lady apologized.

"I'm Rita Lance, an intake worker; this is a ten week program that pays minimum wage until we place you and then you'll make ten dollars an hour. You will be cleaning offices or retail stores. Does this sound like something you like to do, Ms. Wilson?"

Ten dollars an hour, yes I wanted to do it.

"Yes ma'am."

When I went back to see Terrence, he was a lot friendlier.

"They were impressed with you at the employment agency. The woman said you caught on quickly, and they are expecting to start work next week."

That was good news. That meant ten dollars an hour was coming.

"Do you have the GED information?"

"Yep, right here."

The GED classes up north were a lot different than on Southside. The classes started at the third grade level but moved a lot faster. We were doing high school Geometry, Algebra, and history the third week. But we wrote plays too, and that was the fun part. We wrote a play that won a Pegasus play write award. So, it wasn't all hard boring work.

For the first time, I passed part of the GED test. I got a 100 percent on the Constitution part, and the teachers were sure I would pass the other parts soon.

I was working at night full-time, earning ten dollars an hour and going to GED classes in the morning. I opened a bank account and saved all the weekly checks the agency gave me because that was what Terrence suggested I do. He reminded me that once I turned twenty-one the agency wouldn't pay rent anymore. I not only saved the agency money, but I managed to save money out of my paychecks too.

I dreaded turning twenty-one because I didn't know if I could make it on my own.

When I went to see Terrence about my concerns he told me, "You are already doing it, relax you will be fine."

"But, what if I get fired or something?"

"Then you will have to find another job, like everybody else in society. You are ready, Shanna."

CHAPTER 32

Anything Worth Working For, Is Worth Having

I survived turning twenty-one. This meant that I was no longer a ward of the state, and I was on my own. Having money in the bank stopped my panic. Besides taking the GED test, and using drugs again, becoming homeless was my biggest fear. It paralyzed me, but twenty-one came and went, and I still had an apartment, a job, and I was closer than ever to passing my GED.

One day while at work, I saw an Ebony magazine with Bill Cosby's wife, Camille. She had on a graduation cap and gown. Camille had graduated from college, and I thought...*she's not twenty-one, she was way older.* I felt like if Camille could accomplish her goals at a later time in her life, why couldn't I? For some reason, Camille on the cover of Ebony stayed with me, as a matter of fact, it was my inspiration to move forward.

In spite of all my worries, I decided to get professional help (a tutor named Gary) to pass the GED test. Gary was Caucasian and short. I felt more confident than I ever had, and it felt good. I was getting closer to my dreams and overcoming my fear. Gary worked with me every day, as a matter of fact, at different hours. When the day came to take the GED test again, I felt that I was well prepared.

"Gary, wish me luck, okay!" I said with excitement.

"You gonna do it this time, Shanna, good luck!" Gary said while dropping me off at the test site.

I went into the class, still nervous, and my confidence went out of the window.

What if I forget everything…? Lord, please let me pass this test this time, I said to myself while looking up to the heavens.

"You may start the test."

When the test was over, I felt relieved and was sure I passed. Weeks went by, and Gary and I waited eagerly for the test results. Gary opened the letter, and he didn't say anything, which made me nervous.

"Ummmm, well, yea baby, you passed." Gary said while turning red with excitement.

"You foreal?" I said with my mouth wide open.

"Here, take a look. In order to pass the test, one must receive a total of 2250 points, and you have 2300. We are going to celebrate!" Gary said while pulling me into his car.

"Where are we going?"

"Where you wanna go?"

"I wanna eat some pancakes," I said with more excitement. "Whatever you want, it's on me!"

While Gary and I were eating breakfast in the afternoon, he blurted out some news.

"You wanna be on the cover of the Tribune newspaper, well, it's sort of like a small version of the Tribune, what do you think?" Gary said while eating his hash browns.

"Wait, you work for the Chicago Tribune?"

"Yes, you were like a special project, a part of my internship completion. Some people are going to call you to set up a place and time where we are going to be photographed and interviewed. This is exciting Shanna, right?"

Gary seemed more excited by the minute. I didn't care that Gary would be recognized for helping an "Urban Youth." I finally passed the GED test. The Chicago Tribune took pictures of me and Gary with my GED certificate in my hand in front of the library where we often met to study.

"Gary, with this G.E.D., I can go straight to college, right?" I said with a gleam in my eyes.

"Yea, but college is hard, really hard, you have to think about that a little longer, Shanna." Gary said with doubt in his voice.

"What do you mean I have to think about going to college?"

"Shanna, I went to college, and it wasn't a joke. You have to be prepared." Gary said while getting agitated.

"I'm ready now, and this is the best time!" I said, ignoring Gary's intimidating words.

When my mind was set on a goal, Gary or anyone couldn't stop me because I saw doors opening up, and I wanted to bust through.

I went to Truman College the next day and filled out the financial aid papers and preregistered for the term.

I had to take pre-requisite classes that weren't counted towards graduation, but I knew I had to start from the bottom. I was ready to take on the world after passing then GED test. My dream, my new goal, was to go to college.

I struggled at first, some of the classes were real hard, but I was rewarded too. I remembered what Malik at the job said about keeping a good GPA. English became a thorn in my side, and I dropped the class four times because I was scared of failing it. But, I did English like I did the GED and used all my past attempts to help me pass the class. When I knew enough, I didn't drop the course.

All my GED attempts put me in the right frame of mind for college. I knew all I had to do was study. No matter how difficult the subject, if I studied, I would get it.

I made the Dean's list almost every semester, and when I graduated Malik and the counselors and staff from the Independence for Youth agency were there. I had an Associate's Degree in Psychology and plans on going to Chicago State University.

I was drug free and living a dream I never thought was possible. I didn't look back much, my eyes kept looking forward.

In 1999, I took the entrance exam for Chicago State University. There was an essay part to the entrance exam, and I got discouraged, until, I saw the subject…Living alone vs. Living with Others. I couldn't believe that I had to write about a subject that I knew all too well, thank you Jesus!

I scored high on the essay/English portion of the entrance exam, but low in Math and Reading, but I was happy that I didn't have to take an English course anymore. Again, I had to take pre-requisite courses, but I was determined to get good grades in all my classes.

In the mist of taking pre-requisite courses, I decided to major in Art with Design. My grades were good from the beginning, and they stayed that way. Before graduation, I received a Merit award from the University.

Sometimes I wonder how I made it through it all. While sitting with my fellow graduates waiting for my name to be called, tears of joy flowed down my face as I listened to Danny Davis' (U.S. Representative for Illinois) commencement speech on life after college. He briefly talked about Harold Washington, who I had the honor of meeting before he died in 1987. The moment was surreal, until my name was called. I received my Bachelors in the Arts in June 2003. My mother and brother attended my graduation, and my son was also there, in the womb. He was born October 10th, 2003.

MY MESSAGE

Living in over twenty-one foster homes made me unstable and jeopardized my relationships, especially with men. Some men took advantage of my situation and my naiveté. Luckily, God had my back. I had no self-identity because I never stayed in one place more than a year during my adolescence. Although the odds were stacked against me to achieve my dreams of going to college, the determination /desire that was bestowed upon me outweighed the negative.

Drugs and alcohol were the only things that soothed my pain from neglect and shame, so I indulged heavily. I realized that the life I was living wasn't what I wanted, but it was hard to change for the better because I was a product of my environments. I can say that, out of the twenty-one Foster homes, Peaches was the most influential because she made me realize that even mothers are not perfect, and they make mistakes. Sometimes inspiration doesn't come from a place you would expect it to come from, like your family.

Inspiration can come from a stranger, or that someone who took the time to see potential in you. I received help from many outside sources and took full advantage of the opportunities, and I benefited tremendously... I'm grateful. God works in mysterious ways, and to me, that means through people you wouldn't expect to help...don't be quick to judge. To all my CHILDREN that are in FOSTER CARE, hold your head up because your future is just as bright as someone whose Parents/Parent didn't abandon them.

Society may label Children that are in Foster Care; IT'S JUST A LABEL. We are more connected to God than anyone because we need him the most... A lot of people don't understand what it is like to be a ward of the state, but I'm a here to tell everyone that it's confusing, and it hurts.

It's confusing because one doesn't know where they are going to live at any giving moment. And the result is the loss of self-identity and esteem. The hurting part is when people reject you because you are... you; it leaves a scar in the heart that is so deep, that maybe time can heal... if you are strong. Some Foster Parents, well, from my experience, MOST are taking Children into their homes for the money and not because they care. People don't realize that children who are in Foster homes come from a bad situation at the start and continue the vicious cycle because some Foster Parents are not investing love into these children.

My advice to new foster parents is...think about what you are getting into, is it because you care, or is it for greed (money)? If the Foster Parent cares, and she/they are investing in a child who thought that no one loved them enough, guess what? Great results happen for the child and you as a Foster Parent; the possibilities are endless. Now, if your reason to become a Foster Parent is for greed, you are devastating the life of another human being and later down the line that child's and your future are in jeopardy.

So, My Children who are presently a ward of the state, be strong, and escape to a positive environment. Yes, there are plenty of youth centers that are interested in YOU. Take advantage of these organizations and build your self-esteem and prepare yourself for college and the world because we are waiting for YOU.

EPILOGUE

My brother, Andrew (the name the hospital gave), in 1974. I've been looking for you, and I need to find you. I love you, your sister. My mother, Clare, has been sober for seventeen years, and we are in contact with each other on a daily basis. Mom, I love you, and I'm proud of you. Carl, my dearest brother, has decided that going in and out of jail isn't the way to live. He has been sober for eleven years. I love you Big Bruh!

And as for me, I've been drug free for sixteen years and counting.